Joy!

SAM GORDON

AMBASSADOR

Joy!

ISBN 1 898787 14 X

Published by
AMBASSADOR PRODUCTIONS LTD.
Providence House
16 Hillview Avenue,
Belfast, BT5 6JR

Contents

DEDICATION

to

John and Jean Blanshard

whose lives

"are filled with an inexpressible and glorious joy" (1 Peter 1:9)

First Word

BY ROGER CARSWELL

A prison, a pen, papyrus and Paul were used by God to produce the great little book of Philippians. It has always been a favourite with Christians. Now, Sam Gordon, in his inimitable way has given the modern day reader a key to unlock Paul's letter. You will enjoy the insight, ideas and outlines which come so readily from Sam's enthusiastically biblical mind.

Books are not only for reading but also for reference. This commentary is not the type to just leave on the shelf, but it is one to read, enjoy and be blessed by. Like the book it commentates on, this volume is "a good read."

Most Christians are aware that joy is a major theme of Philippians, but as you go through this book you will discover there is much more to it than that alone.

The wealth of good teaching and practical outworking of Philippians is waiting to be discovered today. I commend to you this book knowing it will help you to make that discovery.

ACKNOWLEDGMENT

This book has been written in the course of a busy pastoral ministry and at a time when I am looking forward to moving into a wider ministry with the Good News Broadcasting Association. I am, therefore, immensely grateful to my wife, Lois, and to all those in our church family at Bethesda Free Church, Sunderland who expressed an appreciation for these studies when I first shared them on Sunday evenings. My life has been enriched through them and I have been wonderfully blessed as I have mused on the writings of so many others - I owe them an enormous debt - very few of us would claim to be entirely original. I have tried, however, in the process of milking many cows to make my own butter!

Second Thoughts

Joy!

That's the bottom line of this book. It was the surprising theme of Paul's letter to the church at Philippi. It's even more incredible when you realise Paul is not living in five star accommodation in the local Hilton. He's writing from the cramped and sparsely furnished apartment he has rented downtown Rome. He is deprived of his freedom as he is under house arrest. He is chained to a big, burly Roman soldier. Times were tough.

Paul was a political prisoner facing possible execution. His friends in Rome were divided in their attitudes towards his case. He had no mission board supporting him. He had no legal aid society defending him. His back is to the wall. And yet, when he puts quill to parchment, he pens an upbeat letter that is resounding with joy.

We live in a mad, bad, sad world ... Paul would remind us that we can live cheerfully. We can move from the shade into the sunshine when we live in the glow of God's presence. Here is a noble quest for quality living - yes, according to Philippians, we can experience designer label joy. It's more than feelin' good. It's living a life where joy is at a premium.

We unlock the door in these chapters to a treasure house of joy. Paul tells us how to maximise our joy potential - he shows us how we can take the first steps to walking down the road to a radiant life. We are introduced to Jesus for He is the joy of living.

That means:

* When the bubble of your life is about to burst ...
* When you are beginning to ping under the pressure ...
* When it seems as though your get up and go has got up and gone ...
* When rolling out of bed is tougher than jumping into bed ...
* When you're pulling your hair out and screaming at the kids ...
* When two and two don't make four and life doesn't make sense ...
* When you wish you could stop the world and get off but realise you can't ...

Cheer up ... there's joy in Jesus!

It's true, you can be joyful ... even though you are a Christian!

CHAPTER ONE

From my cell to your church

"from there we travelled to Philippi" (Acts 16:12)

Seems pretty obvious, doesn't it? But, getting there, wasn't that simple! Life rarely is. There were many moments of deep uncertainty. There were times when Paul must have wondered, is this really happening to me? They knocked on a number of doors. They stayed shut.

He sensed it was time to move on even though God was blessing his gospel preaching with many conversions. The Christians were being strengthened in their faith and churches were growing daily. He was living on the crest of a wave. The flame was spreading. In his heart, however, he knew God had other ideas.

True enough. He finds himself in Troas, just ten miles down the road from the famous city of Troy, on the west coast of Asia Minor. He settles down for the night. It's been a long day. In the wee hours he had a vision. He saw a man from Macedonia who was pleading *"come over here and help us."* Paul felt this was it. This was the green light for which he had been waiting. And, without a moment's hesitation, off he went.

EUROPE ... HERE WE COME!

They arrived. All four of them - Paul, Timothy, Silas and Luke. And, what a welcome they received! You must be joking ... no-one knew they were coming. They had to find their own way around and do their own thing, this was new territory. They were pioneers.

So, what did they do? On the Saturday they searched for a synagogue. They looked in vain. There wasn't one. There weren't even ten Jewish men to form the nucleus required to constitute such a gathering. Such was Philippi!

They didn't give up. They made their way down by the riverside *"where they expected to find a place of prayer."* Their journey was fruitful as a number of women had taken time out to seek God. Paul wasted no time and pulled no punches in sharing with them the story of God's redeeming love. As he spoke the Spirit of God was working in the heart of one of the ladies. Luke says of Lydia that *"the Lord opened her heart to respond to Paul's message."* The first convert in Philippi was a gentile lady, an Asian on business in Europe.

That was only the start. The ball was rolling. It gathered momentum. Others were transformed by the power of the gospel. Acts 16 is a fascinating account of God at work. A church was born ...

Ten years later Paul drops them a line. He writes them a letter. It's short and sweet. It's magnificent though brief. It is a delightful piece of inspired mail. It contains only 104 verses. You could sit down and read it from start to finish in less than ten minutes. And because the message is so captivating and scintillating it will leave you gasping for breath.

A DYNAMIC DUO

"Paul and Timothy" (1:1)

What a way to commence a letter! It certainly wouldn't happen today. It's not what you would find in the average textbook except that it was the norm in the first century. He signs his name at the beginning rather than at the end. He tells them who he is.

Can you imagine it? It is Sunday morning in the church at Philippi. The secretary stands up before the assembled congregation to tell them what is happening the following week ... and to read them a letter. He tells them it is from a long lost friend. They are sitting in suspense wondering who it is from. Then he drops the name: *PAUL.* That was all they needed, the memories would flood back, the smiles would appear, the eyes might fill up with a few tears, their ears would be cocked, you could hear a pin drop, the mere mention of his name sends a shiver down the spine and the legs turn to jelly.

Ten years ago this man had been among them, as an evangelist and church planter. Ten years ago he had been unceremoniously incarcerated, though he was innocent. Ten years ago they had seen God work in a spectacular manner as people were converted from all walks of life. And now, a decade later, his name pops up again. It's almost too good to be true. How it must have thrilled them.

In his book, *Laugh Again,* Charles Swindoll writes: "like art-loving Italians thrilled by the works of Michelangelo, like sixteenth-century German believers who were inspired by a spokesman named Martin Luther, like nineteenth-century black Americans who grasped at every word from Abraham Lincoln, like twentieth-century patriotic Britons who needed a Winston Churchill to help them hold fast, the people of the church at Philippi respected and needed Paul. He was their founder and friend. He was their teacher, their able and much-admired leader."

This was no one man band. Paul was not in the business of empire building. He also includes Timothy in his initial greeting to the church. Apart from the fact that he was his son in the faith he had also played a major role in Paul's evangelistic outreach. He was a valued member of the team. The folks at Philippi would know him and love him. Very shortly he would be paying them another visit as the personal emissary of the apostle.

Paul and Timothy were a formidable team. They had their individual strengths and weaknesses. They beautifully complemented each other. Each one had a job to do and a unique contribution to make. Neither felt threatened. They had their problems but they worked them through and came out stronger and still smiling. They were the best of friends and an excellent partnership.

BIG NAME or PLAIN MR. PAUL

"servants of Christ Jesus" (1:1)

He was the prince of preachers. He was the man who blazed a trail for God in pagan darkness. He was a missionary to the regions beyond. He took the gospel where man had never taken it before. He held city wide crusades. He planted scores of churches. He was prolific with his pen. He was in great demand across Asia, Europe and the Middle East. Everyone would want his services. Why go for skimmed milk when you can have real cream?

How did he introduce himself? *"Paul a servant."*

What staggering humility! He saw himself as a slave. A bondslave. He is one who would be loyal to Jesus because he really loved Him. He is totally committed to Him with 100 percent allegiance. Humble, yes; but there also is the mark of true greatness. He discovered perfect freedom in willing service. The lesson is clear: you can be too big for God to use but never too small.

He didn't act like a prima donna who had to be worshipped, or a fragile hero who had to be treated with kid gloves. He saw himself as a servant. His name in Latin means *"little"* or *"small"* - he certainly lived up to his name. He wasn't interested in doing the evangelical circuit as a celebrity speaker. He didn't run around the country holding seminars on the *how-to* or *how-not-to* of ministry. He wasn't a full time worker doing a part time job. Nor was his a luxurious lifestyle with all the attendant paraphernalia. He was only a servant. Having said that, no greater honour could have been conferred upon him. Why should he stoop to be a cardboard pin-up only as good as his last sermon? The adulation of an adoring public dies away but the praise of God lives on for ever.

ICONS IN PEWS

"to all the saints in Christ Jesus at Philippi" (1:1)

Nothing could be further from the truth! These were no alabaster gurus sitting on a pedestal. You won't find them cast in marble either. Nor will you see them set in decorative stained glass in some cathedral window. They are not *"do not touch"* statues sitting in some ornate museum.

The people to whom Paul is writing are just ordinary people. They are saints! That had nothing to do with them. It's not their fault. It is God who has set them apart for Himself. He is the One who in grace seized the initiative and titled them because He has a special purpose for them.

They are His exclusive people. And, He is happy to identify them as such.

They have not been canonised but they have been cleansed. They are not super pious elitist individuals who are paid up members of a country club. No! They are everyday people made of the same material as the rest of us.

Servants and saints. The trademark of the people of God. Both reveal to us the distinguishing marks of the real Christian.

MEET THE LEADERS

"together with the overseers and deacons" (1:1)

Paul is introducing us here to the leadership in the local church, the elders and deacons. The former is primarily responsible for the spiritual well-being of the fellowship whilst the latter will take care of the material needs within the company.

Here is the distinctive nature of the church of Christ. It is comprised of saints, ruled by elders and served by deacons. There is no hierarchy but there is an organised structure. It is not a matter of climbing up the ladder to the office of deacon or being promoted even higher upon recognition as an elder. It is not tiered in that sense. Our feet remain on level ground even though our responsibilities may increase. We serve each other.

ENJOY THE BLESSING

"grace and peace to you from God our Father and the Lord Jesus Christ" (1:2)

It is a double-barrelled blessing. The twin towers of the gospel. We have grace and peace. The order is of ultra importance. You can never know peace in your heart without experiencing the grace of God. Peace is a wonderful spin-off from the grace of God. From a different perspective, we can say that grace is the fountain of which peace is the stream.

Paul could not have wished anything better for them. This was the longing in his heart that they might know both blessings. Grace is something that comes to us that we don't deserve and which we cannot repay. Grace stoops to where we are and lifts us to where we ought to be. Peace is something that happens within us, a freedom from inner distraction, an internal rest. Peace is a tranquillity of soul that frees you from fear and takes the sharp edges off your anxiety.

Grace and peace don't come from ourselves, no matter how positive our thoughts; or from others, no matter how assuring their counsel. They come only from God.

Look at it from another angle:

After conducting Beethoven's magnificent *Ninth Symphony,* Arturo Toscanini brought down his baton to a burst of spontaneous applause. The appreciative audience roared its approval. Toscanini and his orchestra took repeated bows. When the cheering finally subsided, Toscanini turned back to his musicians and leaned over the podium. Voicing his words in staccato whispers, he said to the men: "Gentlemen, I am nothing ... Gentlemen, you are nothing ... But Beethoven ... Beethoven is everything, everything, everything!"

Whether it's Toscanini or Paul, whether you're in a cell or in a church, whether you're in Pitlochry or Philippi, these people are nothing. We are nothing. But Christ is everything. When that gets embedded in our minds, we'll just be satisfied to be the least of saints, the foremost of sinners, used in the hands of God.

CHAPTER TWO

Thanks a lot!

The first two words say it all: *"I thank"* (1:3). Paul was showing a spirit of genuine appreciation for them. It was a heartfelt gratitude for their practical fellowship in the gospel. He wasn't flattering them, he was only telling the truth.

There was an affinity that they so obviously enjoyed, a oneness of purpose, a sense of mutual understanding, a bond that binds them together. They really hit it off. They clicked!

And so, when Paul takes a walk down memory lane, he just says *"thanks, Lord, they're a delightful group of people."* They brought a smile to his face every time he thought about them. He had no hangups about his time there. He had no regrets. He nursed no ill feelings. He had no chips on his shoulder. He struggled through no unresolved conflicts. His thoughts were happy and positive. It's obvious that Paul was made for Philippi and that they were good for him. That's what happens when you have a round peg in a round hole. It's a natural fit!

THERE'S LIFE

Ah, now we know why Paul felt the way he did! The answer is found in 1:7 where we read: *"all of you share in God's grace with me."* They had something in common, it was an experience of the wonderful grace of God.

As individuals, they had been to Calvary, they discovered the ground was level at the foot of the Cross, they had been to an empty tomb, they had fallen prostrate before the throne of the Lamb glorified in heaven - that's what forged a kindred spirit. To borrow the phrase from Jude 3, they shared *"a common salvation."* At the very heart of their relationship with each other was the realisation that they were but sinners saved by the grace of God. They were beggars sharing the same loaf of bread.

There they were, sharing the same life, bound for the same destination, serving the same Lord - *"participators in the divine nature"* - that is what joined their hearts together.

Yes, it's true: they had their differences of opinion, they had many difficulties to overcome, they had major problems that needed to be sorted out, they had their individual personalities; but, in spite of these, and in spite of each other, they were one in Christ.

The fellowship they experienced was not shallow or superficial. It was rich. It was real. It cemented their lives together. There was a deep sense of unity in the Spirit. There was a cohesive bond that they dearly treasured. They were in it together! Partners in *koinonia!* Their brand of fellowship was an expression of vibrant, authentic Christianity in action.

You see, it is apparent from chapter one that their *fellowship* in the gospel (vs.5), promoted the *furtherance* of the gospel (vs.12), and it guarded the *faith* of the gospel (vs.27).

Seems incredible ... but, remember, that's the way it was. Look at some of the foundation members. They were as different as chalk and cheese. On the face of it there would seem to be nothing that would cause them to gel. It was all sorts of people, they were a mixed bag! On a purely human level, you wouldn't find them living on the same street, let alone find them worshipping in the same church ... and enjoying it!

Lydia was there! She was a wealthy businesswoman from Thyatira who had made her fortune from selling purple cloth. She was obviously well heeled and upper class and would have climbed the social ladder. Her's was a lifestyle of affluence ... she didn't receive any special grade of life more suited to her bank balance!

The anonymous slave girl was there! This poor soul is a pathetic sight - she was demented, degraded and demon possessed. She lived her life in the gutter and sold her body so as to scrape together a meagre existence. For her, life was hardly worth living ... she didn't receive an inferior quality of life just because she was a street woman from the slums!

The jailer was there! He was on the brink of committing suicide before Paul talked him out of it. He lived his life on a knife edge because of the responsibility resting on his shoulders and because of the uncertain whims of his employers. He was a decent sort of bloke earning a good wage. He was a family man ... just because he was who he was he didn't get anything different in terms of the package offered to him at his conversion.

No! The life given to all three of them was exactly the same, the grace experienced by each of them was precisely the same, the Lord they trusted was the same person ... that's what we need to remember: no matter who we are, no matter what we are, no matter where we are from, the life we have in Christ is the same for every member in God's global family. We are in the eyes of God on an equal footing! He does not make fish of one and flesh of another. Favouritism isn't in the divine vocabulary. Thank God, He makes no difference. Why should we?

Can you imagine it? Lydia standing at the kitchen sink washing the dishes after a fellowship meal ... *why not?* The slave girl standing at the front of the church leading the people in a time of praise and worship ... *why not?* The jailer standing in the vestibule greeting everyone who turns up for worship with a warm handshake or perhaps a holy kiss ... *why not?*

This is the essence of life in Christ! Discrimination in God's family is neither politically correct nor spiritually sensitive. It is a no-go area. As far as Paul was concerned, it was a non-starter.

THERE'S LOVE

When you receive the life of Christ you also receive the love of Christ. Paul uses three thoughts to underline this particular truth. He says first of all:

I think about you (1:3)

He is jubilant as he reminisces of his time spent in Philippi. When Paul quietly reflects on those early days his heart is filled with gladness and his mind is uplifted. I find it quite remarkable, that even when he is housebound, Paul is thinking of others not himself. And, every recollection he has brings him incalculable joy and pleasure. Precious memories.

There was much that happened to Paul in Philippi, the memory of which could produce considerable pain and sorrow. It seems, the Lord in His grace and tenderness had healed his damaged emotions and had enabled him to cope with such times when life didn't seem fair. Sometimes bad things do happen to good people.

He was illegally arrested and hauled before the court on trumped up charges. Both he and his companion, Silas, were *"severely flogged"* before being *"thrown into prison."* They were apparently a security risk so they were put in the *"inner cell"* and fastened to the stocks. It was the ultimate in humiliation and horror. Even those memories brought joy; it was through his suffering that the prison warder and his immediate family found Jesus as Lord and Saviour. God works in strange ways! Paul had learned to look on the bright side because he knew God was in control of every situation. He discovered the value of viewing events on earth from the perspective of heaven. In the light of eternity his trials fade into oblivion.

I care for you (1:7)

This is something so much deeper. It is possible to have people on our minds without having them in our hearts. He not only thinks about them but he feels for them. Paul is saying, in effect: *"As I share with you my feelings, I open my whole inner being to you and tell you that the level of my affection is deep and tender."* Paul wasn't curious. There's a vast difference between putting your nose in other people's business and putting your heart into their problems. He cared!

His sincere love for them was such that it could not be disguised or hidden. His compassionate care was born out of a bona fide concern. Love is the tie that binds. It's not just a select few who he feels this way about, an exclusive handful; no, it is *"about all of you."* There are no exceptions. He doesn't have the clique mentality. His love embraces every single person in the assembly: the good, bad and indifferent.

How does he do it? It was *"the affection of Christ Jesus"* (1:8) channelled through Paul to them. He loved them for the sake of Jesus. He loved them because of Jesus. He loved them through the Lord Jesus. It actually means that he has a passion for them. The burden of them upon his heart is such that his heart aches for them. That's love with a capital L. It is frontline love.

I pray for you (1:4)

The proof that they meant so much to him is seen in the fact that he prays for them and when he does it is *"always with joy."* He has a prayer list and their names are near the top. They are often times targeted at the throne of grace and that is what strengthened their bond of fellowship. Paul thought about and cared for them in the most profound way. He prayed for them.

How easy it is to pray for people who give us reason to be grateful! They often prove to be accepting and affirming, real instead of phony, and supportive and giving rather than subversive and grabby.

Prayer enabled him to cross the miles from where he was to where they were. Paul is a sterling example of an intercessor. He was off his seat and on his knees making contact with God on their behalf. He had the ear of God.

THERE'S THE LORD (1:6)

Paul exudes confidence when he says: *"he who began a good work in you will carry it on to completion until the day of Christ Jesus."* Here is a relationship where the Lordship of Christ is of paramount importance, a fellowship where the Lord is central. God has an agenda and He is sticking to it. He will not be blown off course.

One of the unsurpassed joys of Christian ministry is the anticipation of what the church will ultimately become. A look at the church today can be disheartening and discouraging, but a look at what the church will become is exciting. This was Paul's focus. This was his honest conviction.

The intention here is to show that God is at work. It is an ongoing work. It was something God initiated, it is something which He continues to be involved in, and it is something which one day He will bring to a grand finale. Paul describes it beautifully when he says it is *"a good work."* The Greek word *agathon* ("good") can also be translated *"noble."* So, from start to finish, salvation is a noble work.

The goal is our glorification. It is the moment when we shall be like Him. When Christ gets involved in a person's life He wants to finish what He has started. He commences in order to continue; He continues in order to complete! The end product of a redeemed life is another person in the image of God. The finished work of the Lord Jesus is another sinner who has been transformed into a replica of Christ Himself.

We can look at it like this: I am not what I used to be; and, I may not be what I ought to be; but, praise God, I am not yet what I am going to be!

At home we have a magnet attached to the fridge door. It reads: *Be patient, God's not finished with me yet!* It's true. God hasn't written me off. He has not ditched me. He has not sidelined me. He just keeps on working in my life. He chisels away at the rough edges of my faith and character. He takes the raw material at His disposal and shapes it into a life that is commendable to Him.

Michelangelo, it is said, was walking past a discarded piece of marble when he exclaimed, "I see an angel in there!" His genius could see the potential others had overlooked. Similarly, as Paul has been reminding us, Christ can see possibilities in us. He can see what we can be tomorrow.

Another story is told of a painter who saw a beggar whose clothes were tattered, hair unkempt, and his face dirty. The artist decided to paint the man as he might have looked if he had had the dignity of a job and home. When he invited the beggar to see the painting, the beggar did not recognise himself. "That's me?" he asked. "Yes," said the artist, "that's what I see in you." For the first time in years the aging man was given hope. He promised, "By God's grace I'm going to be the kind of man you see me to be!"

Take heart! God is on the ball. And, He hasn't kicked it into touch! When He does, the final whistle will have blown, the game will be over ... and, believe it or not, we will be perfect!

CHAPTER THREE

Jesus is the Joy of Loving

Some time ago I was given a copy of the book penned by a former chaplain to the United States Senate. Richard C. Halverson writing in *No Greater Power* has this to say:

> Crush marbles and you get fragmentation, disintegration - hard, sharp pieces. You can get hurt if you're not careful.
>
> Crush grapes and you get fragrant, refreshing wine.
>
> *Some people relate like marbles.* The fear of vulnerability hardens them. They protect themselves, allow no-one to penetrate. Being vulnerable is high-risk, and they want low-risk. They bump against others and ricochet around, never enjoying a vital relationship. In brittle lovelessness, they shatter when crushed, and hurt others.
>
> *Some people relate like grapes.* They yield to pressure. They accept their weakness as essential to intimacy. They give love, knowing love is always vulnerable, knowing love is the heart and soul of our faith. When crushed, they bring blessing: fragrant, redemptive blessing.

This was what was happening to the Christians in Philippi. Like a cluster of grapes they were caught in the winepress of trial and affliction. They yielded to God. Consequently, their lives exuded a wine full of faith and fragrant with love. Paul is not talking primarily in verses 9 to 11 about their trials and troubles but he is homing in on their love.

They were not sour in their attitude to the Lord. They were the epitome of sweetness. There was love being manifested in their relationships with other people. There was a sense of commitment to each other in the local assembly of the Lord's people. Paul says *"that's good, now, let's see if we can do better!"*

He tells them the substance of his prayer in verse 9. He prays for them, *"that your love may abound more and more in knowledge and depth of insight."* Quite specific, isn't he? This is quality love. It is nothing but the best. It is not something hollow or superficial. Neither is it a shallow form of sentimental emotionalism. It is spiritual love, *agape* love; it is divine love. This is the kind of virtue that is geared to the other person's highest good. It does not think "what can I get out of this?" On the contrary, it will seek to enhance the other person's life to such a degree that they will pause and give thanks to God for such a display of love with no strings attached. This is John 3:16 love ... Calvary love.

You can hear Paul pray. You can feel his heart beat. You can sense the intensity of his longing as he yearns for their maturity. He wants them to grow. This love is governed by four influential factors ...

IT IS DYNAMIC

They already had love, and Paul desired a greater expression of it. He was not content with what was present already, he wanted more! He didn't want them to rest on their laurels and settle down in middle class comfort.

He longed for their love to abound. The Greek word has the idea of "overflowing, wave upon wave, cascading like a waterfall." What a picture of love in action, it's the Niagara syndrome. This kind of love cannot be measured or contained, it overflows. It is a love that is unrestricted and unrestrained, you can't keep it back, but as we shall see in a moment, you can direct its course.

Paul is careful in his choice of words. When he used the word *"abound"* he was referring to the *extent* of their love in that it should be reaching out to many more people. When he added the words *"more and more"* he was drawing attention to the *effectiveness* of their "outreach." He wanted them to learn how to love more people and love them all better.

It's a matter of improving the quality of our service. It's how we do it.

Abounding love cannot be bound. It is not confined to those we like, or those who like us, or even those we would like to have like us! It is not selective. It does not require an assurance that it will be reciprocated. Yes, we can love the lovely, the lovable and the loving; but, this brand of love, embraces all men. This love is wide enough to love the unloved and the unlovely.

IT IS DISCERNING

The love that we are thinking about here is a love that blossoms best when it is regulated. Paul talks about *"knowledge and depth of insight."* That suggests it not only involves the heart but the mind as well. When the heart and mind are in harmony you have discerning love and loving discernment.

Love grows best in the soil of knowledge. It's not a matter of letting our heart rule our head, far from it. Our love will be controlled by the Word of God, it will be dictated by the parameters of Scripture. The love that we exercise toward others will be synchronised with the teaching of the Lord Jesus. This is a love that knows!

Paul also qualifies his comments with the phrase *"depth of insight."* Real love is not blind! Genuine love will not deaden our critical faculties. It will have 20/20 vision. It is perceptive and will meet the needs of others by conforming to the truth.

He goes a step further down the road in verse 10 by saying: *"so that you may be able to discern what is best."* Most of us would have little difficulty deciphering what is the difference between good and bad; but when you narrow it down to a higher level of better and best it is not quite so easy.

Our goal here is excellence. This love based on real knowledge and keen insight will enable us to assess every situation that presents itself to us. We will have a type of spiritual radar that will equip us to evaluate and make a right and proper decision. Approval will only be given to that which is glorifying to the Lord. This will result in us being able to focus our time and energy on what really counts instead of being hijacked into a game of trivial pursuits. It's all about priority living.

IT IS DISTINCTIVE

Paul's aspiration for the Philippian believers is that they *"may be pure and blameless until the day of Christ"* (1:10).

There are two sides to this one coin, the first speaks of purity. The baseline here is personal integrity. Paul pulls no punches when he says the emphasis here is on the genuineness of the people who are involved in this expanding programme of love. It means we should be whiter than white. Our lives should be above and beyond reproach. There should be an openness and a transparency about our lives. We may not opt to live in a glasshouse but people should be able to see through us. We should have nothing to hide, no skeletons in the closet. Sincerity will be the hallmark of our lives. When our lives are exposed to the bright rays of sunlight there should be no telltale cracks of hypocrisy. That means we will be on the inside what we appear to be on the outside. There will be a ring of reality to all that we profess. Our actions will not be a contradiction of our words.

The poet put it like this:

> Be who you is,
> because if you is who you ain't,
> you ain't who you is.

It may have a minimum of eloquence but it maximises common sense. And, it is powerfully true!

The second facet speaks of living a life that is *"blameless."* This is descriptive of relational integrity. It means living a life that doesn't cause others to stumble. In all my dealings in love with other people and groups I should seek to be a stepping stone rather than a stumbling block.

Ironically, the Greek word employed here is *skandalon*. Originally it referred to the part of a trap to which the bait was attached. If a person is an offence, he does that which causes another to fall into one of Satan's traps. Paul's desire was that these believers would live so that no one would ever stumble because of their behaviour.

The apostle reminds them of the approaching *"day of Christ"* as an incentive to be known as men and women of integrity. This is a reference to the day when believers will stand before the judgment seat of Christ for the purpose of assessment. It is the day when our lives will come under the searching scrutiny of our blessed Lord. This is the moment when after a personal interview with Jesus rewards will be handed out to those who have been loyal and faithful to Him.

The lesson is clear: we are responsible down here, and, we are accountable over there!

IT IS PRODUCTIVE

He brings his prayer to a conclusion on a typical high note when he writes of them being: *"filled with the fruit of righteousness that comes through Jesus Christ - to the glory and praise of God"* (1:11).

Paul is not principally interested in activity but in the kind of spiritual fruit that is yielded when we are in fellowship with the living Christ. It is God who produces this kind of fruit in the life of the Christian, the secret is our abiding in Christ (cf. John 15). When we do we will bear *fruit* (John 15:2), *more fruit* (John 15:2), *much fruit* (John 15:5), and *much more fruit* (John 15:8). Our lives will be richly productive!

What is the fruit He longs to see reproduced in us?

There is the *fruit of the Spirit* that we read of in Galatians 5:22,23 which is a balanced, healthy life that resonates to the praise of God. Paul compares winning people to Christ as bearing fruit (cf. Romans 1:13; 15:28). We are exhorted to *"bear fruit in every good work"* (Colossians 1:10) and *"to offer to God a sacrifice of praise - the fruit of lips that confess His name"* (Hebrews 13:15).

Fruit, therefore, comes in all shapes and sizes. When our faith works and our love is abounding then a harvest is inevitable. And, God is glorified.

Then, Paul's prayer will have been answered in their lives. Will it be answered in your life and mine?

CHAPTER FOUR

What's happening?

Paul deserves a medal!

Why? What's so special about him?

Let him speak for himself. This is what he says: *"now I want you to know, brothers, that what has happened to me has really served to advance the gospel"* (1:12).

Superb, isn't it! He knows how to handle himself in the good times as well as in the bad times. When everything seemed to be falling apart he sensed that God was still in control. When all he had was a handful of shattered dreams he still believed that God would make Romans 8:28 a living reality. Life for Paul, from a human perspective, had taken a dramatic downturn. Even to a seasoned optimist it would still appear as though he was destined for a rough ride on the roller-coaster of life. Alas, he is finding out quickly, that life is no joy ride. His life seems to be collapsing around him like a pack of cards. This was an abrasive rub with reality.

When you take the lid off the phrase, *"what has happened to me,"* it appears as though the dominoes are falling all around him. Yet, because of his attitude, he smiles through suffering. His outlook shows us how we can make the best of times out of our worst of times. The pain is taken out of his adversity because he trusts God implicitly. His understanding of Providence was not airy-fairy, it was earthed in personal experience. Even though the tapestry of his life seems to be no more than a collection of twisted knots, he doesn't start questioning, *"Why? Why this? Why me? Why now?"*

He knew what he was talking about. It wasn't out of the top of his head. This was life, real life, life in the raw. It's not unlike the stirring testimony of Betsie Ten Boom as she lay dying in the Ravensbruck Concentration Camp. She uttered a sentence which has travelled around the world. "There is," she said, "no pit so deep that Christ is not deeper still." Beaten by a Nazi rifle, humiliated by the Holocaust, she said to her sister, "They will listen to us because we have been here."

The six million dollar question is: what happened?

Paul had one all-consuming passion. He wanted to go to Rome. Not just to see the sights. But to tell Nero and his fellow citizens of his encounter with the living Lord. Rome was comparable to the Oval Office of the world, the place of ultimate clout. As Warren Wiersbe succinctly comments, "he wanted to go to Rome as a *preacher*, but instead he went as a *prisoner*."

Actually, it all began to go wrong when he arrived in Jerusalem. He was illegally arrested. He was falsely accused and nearly lynched by a religious mob of fanatical extremists. They were baying for his blood, they thought the only good preacher was a dead one. They told him he was someone that he wasn't, an Egyptian renegade high on their wanted list (cf. Acts 21:38). He became a political football kicked all over the place, he was moved from pillar to post. He was like a spider caught in the web of politics, he was enmeshed. There was one court appearance after another. And then, he was given a complimentary single ticket for a cruise across the Mediterranean. There was a storm, *"a wind of hurricane force,"* that caused the ship to run aground off the island of Malta. Three months and a few days later he reached Rome. He was imprisoned and for two years he was virtually forgotten as he waited for the outcome of his appeal. The odds seemed unbeatable.

One of the most challenging assignments for any of us is to interpret the tragedies of life in such a way that they become bearable. If only we could read God's diary; if only we could understand His hidden purposes!

That's what happened to Paul!

It would have been natural for Paul to have reacted in an aggressive manner to all the mishaps in his life, it just seemed as though everything was going wrong. He could have kicked the garden fence and vented his spleen on a punch bag. Or, he could have put the blame fairly and squarely on other people. In so doing he would have left himself wide open for blackmail from the adversary himself. He would only be hammering a few nails in his own coffin as the root of bitterness would surely entwine itself around his heart.

Or, he could have wallowed in the slough of despond and become depressed and immobile. Like quicksand, he would be sucked under by his circumstances. I imagine another knee-jerk reaction would be for him to postpone his feelings. It's the Scarlett O'Hara syndrome: "I'll think about it tomorrow." He could let it simmer by placing it on the back burner over a low flame. On the surface all seems calm; but underneath, his feelings seethe.

He didn't react in any of those ways. Thankfully! He had an alternative.

Says Paul, *"alright, it's bad, but it's not the end of the world! It could have been worse, well, it could have been!"*

He realised that God has His agenda for each of our lives. From this most harrowing experience he instinctively says in a voice etched with sincere conviction: *"it has really served to advance the gospel."* That's the spirit, man. That's the way to look at it. Never say die!

He's not licking his wounds in a corner. He's not sulking because he is confined to barracks. He's not feeling sorry for himself. He doesn't feel inconvenienced at all. He doesn't give me the impression of a man coming apart at the seams because of the intolerance of a repressive regime. Far from it!

He is buoyant in his faith and relishing the opportunities that God in His unique way has brought to him. He doesn't have to go looking for a congregation, they come to him!

We read, *"as a result, it has become clear throughout the whole palace guard and to everyone else that I am in chains for Christ"* (1:13).

For twenty four hours a day he was chained to a Roman soldier. Every six hours the shift changed. So Paul had four potential prospects for salvation every day of the week. During his two year internment that meant he would have no fewer than 3,000 witnessing opportunities. Terrific!

He may have been locked up but he wasn't tongue tied when it came to sharing his faith in Jesus. Paul was in his element, he had a captive audience. They had no option but to listen. They couldn't help but hear what he said. And the outcome was such that some of these crack imperial troops were gloriously converted.

The gospel had triumphed. It had made an inroads into the heart of Rome itself. Phenomenal. But, that's how Paul saw it. The Greek term he used to describe it is most colourful. It was used in ancient times to describe a group of pioneer woodcutters who preceded an advancing army, clearing the way through an otherwise impenetrable forest of trees and underbrush; it is a military term that was used by engineers who would prepare a road for an advancing army by removing all obstructions. Paul viewed his circumstances as having cleared the way for the gospel to advance into the nerve centre of the vast Roman empire. This was no setback. It was progress. It may have been a small step for Paul but it was a giant leap forward for the gospel of Jesus Christ.

Paul, in the cold light of day, reflects and says: *"because of my chains, most of the brothers in the Lord have been encouraged to speak the word of God more courageously and fearlessly"* (1:14). There is always the ripple effect. Others are influenced by our lives more than we realise sometimes. This was the impetus some of them needed to engage in the cut and thrust of personal evangelism. It added a new dimension to their ministry. There was a boldness to their witnessing that was not there before. It gave a sharp cutting edge to their proclamation of the gospel message.

The hymnwriter draws the threads together with the conclusion that: *God moves in a mysterious way, His wonders to perform.* What does it matter so long as God moves? I am attracted by the comparisons made by Warren Wiersbe when he says, "the same God who used Moses' rod, Gideon's pitchers, and David's sling, used Paul's chains."

THE MESSAGE IS BIGGER THAN THE MAN

Paul is not looking for sympathy because of the restrictions he is facing nor is he so insular that he can't be rational about what is happening on the outside. He knows there are those who are out to do him harm, there are others who are loyal in their support of him. Some are determined to add high octane fuel to the fiery trial he is experiencing, they don't really care about him as a person. They were taking advantage of his situation and *"stirring up trouble for him while he was in chains"* (1:17). Paul chose not to dwell on what they did to him. We don't know exactly what it was and it is a fruitless exercise to engage in speculation. Whatever it was, they did him no favours! He was not desensitised as a person, he had his feelings and he must have been hurt by their actions. They were adding insult to injury as they poured salt upon his wounds.

Stuart Briscoe describes Paul like this: "Whatever we may think of Paul, he had a temper that got heated and feelings that got hurt. He was no computerised theological machine churning out inspired writings, but a very warm human individual who needed as much love as the next man, and then some. You can't hurt a computer's feelings or grieve a theological concept, but you can destroy a man. Paul was destructible, but he wasn't destroyed. And it wasn't for lack of somebody trying! The perspective that he had discovered allowed him to say that he didn't really mind what happened to him so long as nothing happened to stop the gospel, because in his understanding the message preached mattered more than the man preaching."

It wasn't who was doing it, it was the way they were going about it. That was what really bothered him. Some were preaching Christ *"out of envy and rivalry"* (1:15). As Paul described those who were preaching for the wrong reasons, he used an interesting word. He said they were preaching *"out of selfish ambition"* (1:17). It has the idea of "canvassing for office in order to get people to support you." It was party politics! They were jockeying for positions of influence within the local Christian community. They were wheeler-dealing in all kinds of behind closed doors clandestine manoeuvres. Their aim was to get people to follow them; Paul's goal was to get people to follow Jesus Christ. What a difference!

Paul plainly asks the question: *"But what does it matter?"* (1:18). He wasn't going to get dragged into throwing mud at people especially those who professed faith in his Lord and Saviour. It deeply concerned him but he didn't lose any sleep over it. It wasn't worth it, and neither were they. He had other ways of expending his energy instead of wasting time in a war of words with them. Arguing with them would achieve little or nothing. Paul was walking on the proverbial tightrope. He maintained his sense of balance by keeping his eyes on the Lord. These folks were a minor distraction. Maybe a slight irritation. That was all.

All that mattered to Paul was that *"Christ is preached"* (1:18). And He was! Paul was happy with that even though he did not approve of their motives. He has a big heart and a pair of broad shoulders. He would take it on the chin even though it was designed to knock him out of action.

The message is bigger than the man! God may bypass the man but He will always bless the message of Christ and Him crucified.

CHAPTER FIVE

On the winning side

There is a story about a monastery in Portugal perched high on a 300 foot cliff. It can be reached only by a terrifying ride in a swaying basket. The basket is pulled with a single rope by several strong men who labour as they pull their cargo up the sheer cliff. One tourist became nervous as he began the journey because he noticed that the rope was old and frayed. "How often do you change the rope?" he shouted to the monk as the trip up the mountain began. "Whenever it breaks!" came the reply.

Spine chilling! It doesn't bear thinking about, does it? The small print on the insurance policy would hardly encourage such a journey. Nevertheless, assuming the rope is in good condition, there should be no problem. The onus is on those who are holding the ropes ...

This is what Paul is drawing attention to in 1:19 when he says with candid comment: *"for I know that through your prayers and the help given by the Spirit of Jesus Christ, what has happened to me will turn out for my deliverance."*

MEN ARE PRAYING

He sees his ultimate deliverance as being dependent on two factors. There is the human input into his situation and there is the divine touch upon his life. Through their prayers they are holding the ropes! He valued and treasured their prayerful interest and support enormously. It meant so much to him to have the assurance that they were upholding him before the Throne. Oh yes, he had prayed for them, now it was his turn to be on the receiving end. The ball was now back in his court. And, he was elated and humbled at the same time. What he himself practised in his own life, he also profited from as it was lived out in others.

This is what kept him going, it made all the difference in his outlook. It was the silver lining to the cloud of his confinement. Because he was the focus of their prayers he was able to survive this particular crisis. Many of us have discovered it can make all the difference between us hangin' in there or us calling it quits.

GOD IS PROVIDING

Not only was Paul sustained by the prayers of the saints but he was also encouraged by the provision of the Spirit. The language that Paul is using here is picturesque, the phrase literally means, *"the full supply of the Holy Spirit."* All the resources that heaven could muster were made freely available to Paul. There was no lack in God's supply, it just kept on flowing his way. It was lavish. It was generous. It was just what he needed and more.

Paul is quietly confident because he knows that God will continue to order the events in his life. He places himself at His disposal. All these are links in the chain that will bring about his deliverance, in His time. For Paul, it is one day at a time. That's enough for any man to think about. He knew that he would come through his ordeal with their prayers and with the help of the Lord. He knew what he was experiencing was not the end, it would all turn out exactly as God directed.

Things are not always as they seem. *Let me illustrate:*

A shipwrecked man was once washed ashore on an uninhabited island. In the days that followed he painstakingly constructed a hut with a few things he salvaged from the wreck and from whatever he could find on the island. That little hut was the only protection he had from the harsh elements and the only place he could safeguard his possessions.

Upon returning one evening from a lengthy search for food, he was terrified to find the hut engulfed in flames. The loss devastated him. He spent that night despondent, sleeping on the sand.

He awoke early the next morning and, to his surprise, saw a ship anchored off the island. A crew member stepped ashore and told him, "We saw your smoke signal and came to rescue you!"

What seemed to be destruction turned out to be deliverance. The same would be true of Paul in Rome. God would work it all out! He needed to learn the lesson that we all need to grasp at times: when all seems lost, it isn't.

THINKING TODAY ABOUT TOMORROW

With such a mindset Paul continues to focus on the future. He is forward looking and planning ahead as he anticipates the day of his release. He says, *"I eagerly expect and hope"* (1:20). What a fantastic comment to make, it is one of eager expectation! The Greek word actually has three elements wrapped up in its meaning. It is comprised of the words "away," "the head," and "to watch." When you put them all together, they convey the idea of watching something so intently that your head is turned away from everything else.

It's the single mind syndrome. It's the *"this one thing I do"* philosophy favoured by Paul and his erstwhile contemporaries. It's all about setting a goal and going for it. His vision is not blurred. His sense of destiny has not diminished. He knows where he is going. And, he'll get there. Typical of Paul, isn't it?

His hope is such that he is sitting on the edge of his seat. He is standing on his toes because his confidence is so high. This spurs him on in his quest to be the kind of person God wants him to be. He doesn't want to have any regrets about his life, *"that I will in no way be ashamed"* (1:20), he wants to have an unblemished and untarnished testimony. Even though the pressure he is experiencing is enough to cause a mental blowout he just wants to please the Lord in all his ways.

The temptation would be for Paul to want to make life easier for himself. It would be easier if he said nothing about his faith. Silence would be golden in the short term. Instead, he prays that he *"will have sufficient courage so that now as always"* (1:20) he will be able to talk about the Lord with boldness. Paul didn't go softly, softly; he turned the volume up louder.

His supreme desire is reflected in the words that flow graciously from his quill on to the parchment. He longs that *"Christ will be exalted in my body, whether by life or by death"* (1:20). This was all that mattered to Paul. It was the driving force in his life on planet earth. Irrespective of where he was, in a prison or in a pulpit, in a cell or in a church, anywhere and everywhere, he just wanted his Lord and Saviour to be glorified in his body. If that meant life, great! If it spelt death, so what? From Paul's point of view, Jesus Christ is unrivalled.

What starts the adrenalin rushing through Paul's veins? What turns him on? Here's the answer: *"for to me, to live is Christ and to die is gain"* (1:21).

Jesus Christ was number one in his life. This was the motivational factor in his ministry, this was the propelling thrust in all that he sought to do. No wonder his life had such power and momentum. Someone has said, "he forced every experience of life through the grid of his personal purpose statement." Here is the secret to living well and dying well. It's all down to the reality of our relationship with Jesus Christ. In the final analysis, when all is said and done, it's all about the centrality of Christ in the life of the individual.

We will take the liberty and reword the verse like this ... see if it makes sense to you. This is the acid test of our consecration to Christ:

* for me to live is *money* ... and to die is to leave it all behind.

* for me to live is *fame* ... and to die is to be quickly forgotten.

* for me to live is *power* ... and to die is to lose it all.

* for me to live is *things* ... and to die is to go empty handed.

All of these fall flat, don't they? They fly in the face of contentment and happiness. They don't bring lasting joy. Only *Christ* can satisfy, whether we have or don't have, whether we are known or unknown, whether we live or die!

TO GO OR NOT TO GO

Talking about life and death, Paul has a problem. It all becomes a little complicated. He is on the horns of a dilemma. He can't make up his mind. He doesn't know what to do, to do what is best for himself or to do what is more beneficial for them. He was caught between his desire to be with Christ personally and his sense of duty to help the Christians at Philippi. He was between a rock and a hard place, or as he put it, *"torn between the two."* He's in a real quandary as he faces such a titanic struggle. It is not a matter of pulling the shortest straw or making a decision based on the toss of a coin. It's not as easy as that!

Here is the line of reasoning that he follows: *"if I am to go on living in the body, this will mean fruitful labour for me. Yet what shall I choose? I do not know! I am torn between the two: I desire to depart and be with Christ, which is better by far; but it is more necessary for you that I remain in the body"* (1:22-24).

What a man! Warren Wiersbe described him well, when he said, "he is willing to postpone going to heaven in order to help Christians grow, and he is willing to go to hell in order to win the lost to Christ (cf. Romans 9:1-3)."

Commitment is the name of the game. Paul was committed to a cause and he was totally committed to Christ. When you look at what Paul is saying you quickly realise that it is not all cut and dried, there are pros and cons either way. Whatever decision is made there would be advantages and disadvantages, at the end of the day he would be cast upon the Lord to lead and guide him in the path of His choosing.

How does Paul talk about death? He depicts it as a *departure*.

It is a most instructive word. It is a word that was used by soldiers, it refers to taking down your tent and moving on to another place. Sailors were also familiar with this expression, to them it meant to loosen a ship from her moorings and set sail. It was also a term used by the judiciary, it captured the moment when a prisoner would be released and set free. The farming community used the saying frequently, it signified the unyoking of a pair of oxen thereby removing their burden.

Death, therefore, held no terrors for Paul. He had nothing to fear or dread. For him it was no more than a change of location because the Lord was with him in either situation. He was on the winning side whatever decision was made. That's what made the question he wrestled with so difficult to answer.

If he stayed, the church at Philippi would reap a handsome dividend, they would benefit from the rich biblical ministry of Paul and from his helpful asides with regard to their particular situation. The church at large would also derive much blessing from his proclamation of the Word of God. The world would certainly be better off because he would be out there with many others preaching the gospel and seeing men and women turn to faith in Christ. He would continue to blaze a trail for God in reaching the unreached with the life giving message of Jesus and His love.

If he went, he would be better off! He would be ushered immediately into the presence of the Lord whom he dearly loved. The trials and troubles of life would be gone. The tears of frustration would all be wiped away. The hassles and niggles of trying to work with so many people all of the time would be at an end. The uncertainties about the future would have evaporated as he entered heaven itself. The limitations imposed by time and circumstance would be forever removed as he walked through the gate into glory. It would be heaven and his joy would be complete!

Paul reached the other side because the folks in Philippi were holding the ropes on his behalf, they prayed for him. Now, when he finds himself at a T junction on the road of life, he hands the reins over to the Lord. The decision is the Lord's. It's better that way, His are a safe pair of hands.

What was it? *"Convinced of this, I know that I will remain, and I will continue with all of you for your progress and joy in the faith, so that through my being with you again your joy in Christ Jesus will overflow on account of me"* (1:25,26).

He was staying, for a little while at least. He was happy to go along with the plan of God for his life. Personal preference was gladly set aside so that the purpose of God might be unfolded. He wanted to go, but he was content to stay. God had a job for him to do. His work was not finished, yet!

CHAPTER SIX

A Call to Arms

Before Andrew Jackson became the seventh president of the United States, he served as a major general of the Tennessee militia. During the War of 1812 his troops reached an all-time low in their morale; a critical spirit grew up among them. They argued, bickered, and fought among themselves. It is reported that Jackson called them all together on one occasion when tensions were at their worst and said: "Gentlemen! Let's remember, the enemy is over *there!*"

It's all about getting along with each other. We can polarise and pay the price *or* we can stick together and win the battle. We can be petty and fragment and back a loser *or* we can pull together in the same direction and back a winner!

Too often we forget the identity of the enemy. He has confused us and sent us into disarray. We are going round in circles. We sleep and he edges forward. We fight among ourselves and he makes strident advances.

The stirring challenge at the end of chapter one of Paul's letter is to head for the front line, get into the trenches, and fight. It is a call to arms.

He reminds them that *"whether I come and see you or only hear about you in my absence"* (1:27) he wants them to be engaged in the conflict of overpowering the enemy. He wants to see their adversary routed and roundly defeated. He knows only too well that if they give him an inch he will take more than a mile, and, as a local fellowship they are only one generation short of potential extinction. It's as urgent as that! Serious stuff!

A PLEA TO STAND

"conduct yourselves in a manner worthy of the gospel of Christ" (1:27)

The emphasis here in Paul's thinking is that we should be willing to stand up and be counted. He's not playing the numbers game. He's not in the business of keeping the statisticians busy either. But he is advocating a distinctive lifestyle for the people of God. We are meant to be different. Not odd! Whether we like it or not, our lives speak volumes to those around us. Our actions speak louder than our words. Our lives are audible, hence the need for consistency.

Someone has said that a man who refuses to stand for something will sooner or later fall for anything. That is why our personal conduct is a matter of mega-importance. It is absolutely essential there should be nothing in our lives that would cause the name of Christ to be smeared.

A godly life, a steady walk with the Lord, a bright testimony and a joy in the heart will all prove to be a potent force in a corrupted world. A person of such ilk is a credit to his Saviour and a challenge to the sinner, it makes them sit up and think about what they're missing.

We are the Bibles the world is reading. I sometimes wonder when they look at my life, what translation it is. You can't beat a life that is consistently lived for Jesus. It is the greatest weapon we have against the enemy. The finest sermon ever preached was entitled: *The Life Lived.* Let's make it personal and ask the searchingly pertinent question, "What is the gospel according to you?"

A PLEA TO STRIVE

There is an intriguing phrase in Paul's letter which hits you between the eyes. It is when he says, *"whatever happens, whether I come and see you or only hear about you ... I will know that you ..."* (1:27). In one sense, he is laying it on the line by telling them that their behaviour should not be dependent on him. If he comes, they should be living a life that will be glorifying to the Lord, and, if he doesn't come, it should make no difference whatsoever. It should not be like the often quoted adage: when the cat's away the mice will play!

They had to learn to stand on their own two feet. It's all about striking a balance between independence and inter-dependence. We are on our own and yet we are in it together! Yes, we need each other in the family, but at the same time, we are expected to live our own lives to the praise of God.

Charles Swindoll with a mix of realism and humour says, "so many live their lives too dependent on others. Such clinging vines draw most, if not all, of their energy from another. Not only is this unhealthy for the clinger, but it also drains too much energy from the clingee!" Enough said.

Having cleared the air as to his position he now moves up a gear by saying: *"stand firm in one spirit, contending as one man for the faith of the gospel"* (1:27).

The stress here is on cooperation. The choice of words is highly suggestive. He speaks about *"contending as one man."* This is the word from which we get our word "athlete." He sees the church as a team and he tactfully reminds them that it is teamwork that secures victories. There are many players but there is only one team.

We should be operating not against one another but for one another. We go forward hand in hand for the greater good of the gospel. We join hands and stand shoulder to shoulder as we engage the enemy in an eyeball to eyeball confrontation. United we stand! Victory is ensured.

Failure to pull together will ensure that the church goes into the hands of the receiver. Its days of usefulness will become a thing of the past.

A PLEA TO SUFFER

There are always casualties on the field of battle. That is part of the price that has to be paid. Suffering is inevitable for those who would be soldiers in the army of the Lord. It is not a question of *"if it comes"* but *"when it comes."* We should expect it and be willing to share in it. When we face it square on then our confidence will grow. It should make us better not bitter. Our spiritual muscle will be stronger and our faith will have more clout in the market place. It will give us street credibility.

Paul warned the Philippians not to be *"frightened in any way by those who oppose you"* (1:28). The natural inclination is to run scared. The word Paul uses here is of a horse shying away from battle or of horses that were so terrified they went into an uncontrollable stampede. That only happens when fear gets the upper hand. The tendency then is to quickly click our heels and not be seen for dust.

This is the only place in the New Testament where this particular word is used, and it is very appropriate for the little group of believers living in Philippi during a violent period of history. It is more than coincidental that Paul addresses them in the manner which he does.

This "courage, brother, do not stumble" attitude in the face of such ruthless oppression and concentrated opposition has a double compensation allied to it. It is a token of their salvation and of their enemies doom - *"this is a sign to them that they will be destroyed, but that you will be saved - and that by God"* (1:28). The sheer inability of their avowed enemies to intimidate them becomes proof of the genuineness of their faith in the Lord. It gives to the casual onlooker and interested spectator an appreciation of what it costs to be a Christian. We don't go looking for a fight but neither do we run away from it.

Paul then adds another dimension to it, he says: *"for it has been granted to you on behalf of Christ not only to believe on Him, but also to suffer for Him"* (1:29). It is patently obvious that believing is the delightful part, suffering is the difficult part. Believing is relatively easy, suffering is intensely hard.

Who likes being persecuted? Who enjoys facing times of hardship and deprivation? Who relishes moments of pain? Who looks forward to days of severe trial and testing?

Probably, none of us! And yet Paul indicates that when we suffer we are doing it for the Lord. It is something which he has *"granted"* to us, it is to be seen as a love-gift from the Lord. We should, therefore, accept it with an overwhelming sense of privilege realising that He knows what is best for us. It is an honour reserved only for those whom He can trust with such an expression of His love.

In a final word of encouragement Paul reminds them that they are not alone in their conflict, he is going through something very similar. He says: *"since you are going through the same struggle you saw I had, and now hear that I still have"* (1:30). The Greek word translated *struggle* here is the term from which we get our word *agony*. It is the identical word that is used in reference to the Lord's critical hour in the Garden of Gethsemane (cf. Luke 22:44). It's not a playground, it's a battle field.

That means, Jesus knows exactly what they are going through and He can empathise with them; Paul can sit where they sit and put his arms around their sagging shoulders and say, "I really do understand because I'm going through the same." They're not alone! And, when it comes to your front door as well as mine, we're not on our own either. At times, it may appear that the Lord is invisible, but He is always invincible. We really are in the best of company. Cheer up!

CHAPTER SEVEN

United we Stand

Stripped naked, falsely accused, humiliated beneath the glare of the lights and the stare of the Gestapo, Victor Frankl stood shaved and shivering in a Nazi courtroom. His shorn head was a symbol of his shorn life; they had stolen his home, his freedom, his possessions, and had even killed his family.

Yet as Frankl faced the men who had robbed him of everything and left him with only years of indignity ahead, he realised there was one thing they could never take away.

His choice of attitude.

He could choose despair or hope, bitterness or forgiveness. He could choose to wallow in self-pity or to endure. The quality of his outer life was beaten into submission, but his inner life was his to rule.

It's all down to our attitude and how we handle what life throws at us.

Another man illustrates the importance of attitude differently - Niccolo Paganini, the gifted Italian composer and concert violinist.

One night, performing before a full house, he began to play a particularly difficult concerto. The audience sat in rapt attention. Suddenly, one of the strings on his Stradivarius snapped, and dangled uselessly beneath his bow.

Perspiration beaded his forehead. He frowned. But he continued to play, his genius lending beauty to his improvisation.

But then, unbelievably, a second string broke. And then a third. Only a single string remained taut, but the great musician finished the piece.

His final notes were swallowed in the wild applause of the audience. As they sank back into their seats, he waved them to silence. With a twinkle in his eye, he shouted, "Paganini ... and one string!" And he lifted his violin and began his encore as the audience shook their heads in amazement.

Again, it's the attitude factor that makes all the difference. He could have gone to pieces and wrecked the performance or carry on as he did with gusto as if nothing had happened.

I came across the two stories outlined above as I was making preparation for this particular chapter. They are a superb illustration of what it takes to be successful in this life, even when we are down to our last string. Like our friend Paganini we need to rediscover that our strength isn't in the number of strings we're playing on, but in the tune we're playing! Yes, it's true, our circumstances aren't always under our control, but our attitudes always are, it's up to us to choose how we think!

Charles Swindoll reckons that "life is 10 percent what happens to us and 90 percent how we react to what happens." He's probably right!

WHEN UNITY BEGINS TO CRUMBLE

How timely then was this message to the church at Philippi. On the whole they were a fairly peaceful, happy group, but apparently there were rumblings going on behind closed doors. From reading between the lines it would seem there were a couple of personality clashes. There were some strained relationships and these were affecting the unity of the fellowship, the lovely feeling of harmony which they previously enjoyed was slowly but surely evaporating. You could sense there was friction in the assembly, there was something not quite right! Feelings were frayed. They were suffering from wear and tear.

Christians, it is said, are a lot like porcupines. They have many good points, but they're hard to get close to. The main reason is that their prickly personalities keep needling each other.

Or, to change the metaphor:

Paul isn't afraid to grasp the nettle. It's a perennial problem and when it gets out of hand it can be an eyesore. So, he reminds them of the beauty and blessings of unity. Be positive. Don't be negative in your outlook.

As a church they had so much going for them, they were a delightful group of people, it was a super fellowship to belong to, it was thriving. Yet, the warning lights are flashing. The smoke signals indicated the presence of a fire. There was something smouldering, a hot potato. Paul hit the nail on the head, he put his finger squarely on the problem: disunity.

There was a ripple on the water, a kind of undercurrent. Now, that's a problem not exclusive to the saints at Philippi; across the world there are many similar situations, at home and abroad so many of God's people aren't getting along with each other. We see it in local companies of the Lord's people, we see it on mission stations dotted across the world. An area of major concern for spiritually sensitive believers is the incompatibility of fellow Christians, they just can't get on with one another. It doesn't say much for the unity of the body of Christ!

WHAT IT IS ... WHAT IT ISN'T

Paul's passionate plea here in 2:1-4 is not for uniformity but for unity.

Uniformity is the result of pressure from without, it's when people want us to conform to their way of doing things. They say, "be like me and do it my way." We dress alike, look alike, sound alike, think alike, act alike, we become spiritual clones.

Unity comes from within and is a matter for the heart. It is experienced when we are conformed to the Lord Jesus. He says, "be like Me and do it My way." It means to be on the same team, going for the same goals, for the benefit of one another.

We are different. We're meant to be different. Yet, we can still be one! We will have our differences of opinion, yet, we can still be one! There is unity in diversity.

TACKLING THE PROBLEM

You will remember that in chapter one of his epistle the theme has been: **Christ first**. The thread woven into the fabric of chapter two is: **others!** Previously he talked about the place he was in, now the emphasis is on the people he is with. Earlier he stressed the need to have a single mind, now he recommends that we have a submissive mind i.e. we will have and hold the mind of Christ. Formerly, he was in the groove of the soul winner, here he is in the mould of a servant.

That, says Paul, is the way forward. We need to see ourselves as nothing more than servants, nothing less than servants, and nothing else but servants. It is all about the attitude of servanthood, a willingness to serve others.

Let's face the facts: there are people we immediately feel at home with, we relate to them easily, we have an instant rapport with them, we just enjoy being with them. There will, however, be those with whom we have a difficult relationship, they seem to rub us up the wrong way, they seem to tramp on our toes especially the ones with corns, we find it hard to relax when they are within earshot, a potential clash is just waiting to happen.

Yes, that's life! Nevertheless, Paul challenges us to pull out all the stops and cause the dulcet tones of harmony to pervade the atmosphere again. It will be like music to the ear and it would *"make his joy complete"* (2:2).

GETTING OUR ACT TOGETHER

"If you have any encouragement from being united with Christ, if any comfort from His love, if any fellowship with the Spirit, if any tenderness and compassion" (2:1)

A plea for unity

He says: "Look, see what you have! Look again, see what you are!"

He gives to the Christians a fourfold incentive to pull together. Here are a quartet of pointers to set them back on the straight and narrow. They have one feature in common: they all begin with *if*. Just because he uses the word *if* does not imply that he is casting doubt upon his own premise, this particular Greek construction is one that assumes that the statement being made is true. It may be better and wiser to translate the phrase with the word *since*. What are they?

* We have union with Christ - that is for our encouragement.

* We are the recipients of His love - that is for our enjoyment.

* We have life in the Spirit - that is for our endowment.

* We have felt His heartbeat - that is for our endearment.

Paul's valiant and vigorous appeal for unity is based not on their feelings about the family, but, on the facts of their faith. These are viable reasons for Christian unity among the people of God.

William Hendricksen summarises it in a most helpful manner when he writes, "The main thrust of what the apostle is saying is this: If then you receive any help or encouragement or comfort from your vital union with Christ, and if the love of Christ toward you does at all provide you with an incentive for action; if, moreover, you are at all rejoicing in the marvellous Spirit fellowship and if you have any experience of the tender mercy and compassion of Christ, then prove your gratitude for all this by loving your brothers and sisters at home."

A path to unity

"then make my joy complete by being like-minded, having the same love, being one in spirit and purpose" (2:2)

Paul says: "this is what you have received, now, share it and show it to others!"

For him, living back in Rome this would be the icing on the cake, it would really make his day into a red-letter day. His cup of joy would be full and running over. What a prayer. What an aspiration. All he wanted was for them to be united, that's all!

He says, "do if for my sake, do it for the Lord's sake, and do it for your own sake."

They were to be *one in mind* - this is a reference to what they believed. It is talking about doctrine and the great tenets of our faith. They were to sign on the same dotted line giving assent to the fundamentals of the faith. There is no spiritual unity without doctrinal oneness. Someone has noted that when it comes to the basis of our faith Christians should be "like clocks that strike at the same moment." The foundation for their unity would be the Word of God.

They were to be *one in heart* - we are to have the same love, not loving the same things but possessing the same love. It is imperative that we show to others that the love of God is flowing in us and through us.

They were to be *one in soul* - it is a most unusual phrase that Paul has coined here but it really conveys the idea of having "joint souls." We are to be soul brothers, in harmony with all of God's people.

Essentially he is saying, "If you want all these things, you can have them, but you'll need to change your attitude and become of one mind. The choice is yours!"

A prescription for unity

Paul is not pussy-footing when he moves into this section. He tells it like it is. He spells out the danger of the "me, myself and I" philosophy. He knocks the grab-all-you-can-get attitude that seems to permeate so much of our thinking in today's world. It's a dog-eat-dog world, they tell you, and the puppies don't make it. We are told if we want to survive that we will need to hold on to the ladder we are climbing for dear life. To succeed, we are advised to claw our way to the top.

He says we are to *"do nothing out of selfish ambition or vain conceit"* (2:3). What a challenge! He is prohibiting a competitive selfish spirit within the church of Jesus Christ. Sadly, this attitude is behind many of the petty squabbles we see in our churches, it's people determined to get their own way so that they can do their own thing. It's riding roughshod over other people. It's a passion to look after number one.

Conceit, on the other hand, means an empty glory. There's nothing to it, and there's nothing in it! It has been likened to a balloon. The larger it stretches on the outside, the bigger the emptiness on the inside. Or, to change the analogy, it is like the empty can that makes the most noise.

The key to unity among the Christian family is to have a spirit of humility. Paul underlines this when he writes, *"but in humility consider others better than yourselves. Each of you should look not only to your own interests, but also to the interests of others"* (2:3,4).

Andrew Murray is credited with this definition: "The humble person is not one who thinks meanly of himself. He simply does not think of himself at all."

Humility is that grace that, when you know you have it, you have lost it!

A humble person is someone who accepts himself for who he is, he is someone who is grateful to God for all that He has done for him, he is an individual who rightly assesses the value of the gifts that the Spirit has given to him. He will not overestimate himself and thereby fall into the snare of pride; neither will he underestimate himself and be caught in the trap of a false humility. His will be a balanced outlook, a Christlike attitude.

He will be people oriented. There will be a willingness and desire to invest himself in the lives of others and go beyond the second mile. People will matter to him, not for what he can get out of them or impart to them, but for who they are! The individual is important in his thinking and in his planning.

It seems to me that when we do what the apostle is asking us to do we will be in a better position to experience the thrill of oneness in the church of Christ.

Unity is available *and* unity is attainable!

How?

By adopting the right attitude.

It is when we extend to our brothers and sisters within the family of God the right hand of fellowship rather than the right fist of fellowship! Maybe we need to link our hearts together more instead of banging heads together. To be united is infinitely better than being untied!

CHAPTER EIGHT

The Way Up is Down

The humorist Mark Twain makes a choice comment when he says with tongue in cheek: "Few things are harder to put up with than the annoyance of a good example."

A good example. You need look no further than Jesus! That is precisely the gist of what Paul is saying: *"your attitude should be the same as that of Jesus Christ"* (2:5). He is an example par excellence of an unselfish outlook. His attitude is such that it automatically puts him in the category of the ideal role model. He is exemplary. He is incomparable. His is a mindset worth embracing and emulating.

What did He do?

He came down from heaven to earth in the greatest stoop of all time. He put His foot on the ladder and stepped down one rung at a time. Don't miss the steps downward:

1. He left the splendour of heaven.
2. He made Himself nothing.
3. He took the nature of a servant.
4. He was made in the likeness of humanity.
5. He humbled Himself.
6. He became obedient to death.
7. He died on a cross.

This is what submission is all about. It's an experience of Calvary in the life of the Christian. It's as personal as it can be and as life changing as it should be.

My heart was moved when I read the words penned by Charles Swindoll in relation to this supreme act of humility and servanthood. He said, "rather than lobbying for His right to remain in heaven and continuing to enjoy all the benefits of that exalted role as the second member of the Godhead and Lord of the created world, He willingly said yes. He agreed to cooperate with a plan that would require His releasing ecstasy and accepting agony. In a state of absolute perfection and undiminished deity, He willingly came to earth. Leaving the angelic hosts who flooded His presence with adoring praise, He unselfishly accepted a role that would require His being misunderstood, abused, cursed, and crucified. He unhesitatingly surrendered the fellowship and protection of the Father's glory for the lonely path of obedience and torturous death."

He did it all. For *you*. For *them*. And, for *me*.

We are staggered with His condescension in 2:5-8 and we are bowled over with His coronation in 2:9-11. His descent from glory is recorded prior to His ascent to the throne. The abiding principle that should dictate our thinking is enshrined in the example of Jesus: the way up is down (cf. James 4:10).

This unbelievable portion in Paul's letter to the Philippians was probably a credal statement used by the early church. It may even have been a hymn that was sung when the Lord's people were gathered together in His name. It is a brilliantly superb masterpiece of Christology, it's all about the Person and Work of the Lord Jesus. It's a rich and unusual combination of meekness and majesty.

The story of the cross is recorded for us in the Gospel narratives and is suitably explained in the Epistles; this, however, is the only place where we are given an insight into what Calvary meant to Him. We see the cross from the perspective of Jesus and through His eyes.

In order to feel the pulse of this remarkable section, I want us to look at the steps that He took as He made the round-trip from glory to glory.

David Jeremiah has a skilfully worded alliterative outline for these few verses. It would be difficult to improve upon his suggested headings. Here they are:

Step one:	**He relinquished His place**
Step two:	**He refused His prerogative**
Step three:	**He renounced His privileges**
Step four:	**He restricted His presence**
Step five:	**He realised His purpose**
Step six:	**He received His promotion**

What are the key phrases that help us open the door into the mind of Christ? Let's try to discover what made Him tick:

"Who, being in very nature God" (2:6)

Here we are confronted with the reality of His deity. We have described here the place of prominence which Christ enjoyed. He and God are One. They are co-equal, co-eternal and co-essential. What One has the Other has, what One is the Other is. He is God through and through. He is all God. He is God. There is not the minutest fraction of Him that is not divine. All that God is, Jesus Christ was and is and ever will be.

"did not consider equality with God something to be grasped" (2:6)

What He often claimed to be was not something which He had pilfered or stolen. What He said about Himself was not something He had gained by false pretences. No! He is equal with the Father. Even though He was God, even though He enjoyed such a favoured position with all its rights and honours, He refused to cling on to these, He was willing to give them up for a season. That is the message of Christ, the Servant King. He surrendered that which He loved in order that He might serve those whom He loved.

"but made Himself nothing" (2:7)

This can be translated "He emptied Himself" or "He made Himself of no reputation." He certainly never emptied Himself of His deity, He was still God at the Incarnation. There were many instances in His life and ministry when He showed His divine attributes in the realm of the miraculous. He became what He never was before, yet, He never ceased to be what He is eternally. It simply means that He laid aside certain rights that were His. He forfeited many of the privileges which were enjoyed by Him in the glory. In emptying Himself He voluntarily stepped from being a Son of the Father in heaven to being the Son of Man on earth.

"taking the very nature of a servant" (2:7)

It's instructive to realise that the same word "nature" is used both here and in the preceding verse. The One who was in the form of God took upon Himself the form of a servant. He was happy to take the place and position of a slave (cf. John 13). The Sovereign assumed the status of a Servant both in nature and by practice. This was the moment when omnipotence surrendered to impotence.

As God, Christ owns everything, but when He became a servant He borrowed everything: a place to be born, a place to lay His head, a boat to journey in, a pulpit to preach from, an animal to ride into a city, a room for the Passover meal, and a tomb to be buried in.

"being made in human likeness" (2:7)

The word "likeness" suggests similarity but difference. Though His humanity was genuine, He was different from all other humans in that He was sinless. He was identified with sinners, He had all the essential attributes of humanity. He was more than God in a body. He became the God-Man. He was fully God and fully Man. He had the same flesh and blood that we have, He knew the limitations of life down here, He was aware of the ups and downs of this life and was subject to all the emotions that mankind faces.

"And being found in appearance as a man, He humbled Himself and became obedient to death - even death on a cross!" (2:8)

Nothing could be more cruel than death on a cross, a person who was crucified died a thousand deaths before finally dying. He was willing to go through with such an excruciating and shameful crucifixion so that we might be set free from the bondage of sin. He lived His life in the shadow of the Cross, from start to finish it was a path of humiliation. This was all part of the Father's plan, the Cross was no accident or afterthought. It was central to the unfolding drama of redemption as revealed in the Word of God.

"Therefore God exalted Him to the highest place" (2:9)

He is where He is today because God placed Him there, He is what He is because God planned it that way. Because of what He did, God moved and did His bit, He exalted Jesus. From out of the depths to the loftiest heights. From the gutters of earth to the glories of eternity. No higher place could be given to Him. He has exalted Him far above all. He's on the top rung of the ladder, He has scaled the summit, He has reached the zenith. The Father welcomed Him back with wide open arms. As He walked along the pavements of Heaven the applause from the angelic band was rapturous and spontaneous.

When we speak of His exaltation we include His resurrection, ascension and coronation. He has sat down at the Father's right hand. He is hailed as a Prince and a Saviour. At His exaltation He received back from the Father all that He laid aside when He came to earth, in fact, He was able to enter into a whole new dimension of ministry as our Great High Priest.

"and gave Him the name that is above every name, that at the name of Jesus every knee should bow, in heaven and on earth and under the earth, and every tongue confess that Jesus Christ is Lord, to the glory of God the Father" (2:9-11)

Paul is here anticipating a future day when men will bend the knee at the mention of His name and also confess that He is Lord. At the appropriate moment all the good angels and the redeemed from all the ages will bow before Him, every inhabitant living on planet earth will bow, and all those under the earth, including all those populating hell together with the fallen evil angels will be required to bow before the Lord of glory.

In that moment, the cycle will have been completed. We will have gone full circle. The One who was humiliated will now be exalted. The One who was brought low will now be raised up high. That's the way it is in the divine economy, the way up is down!

Graham Kendrick has composed a song based on these verses. Think of the words as you read it through for yourself ...

Meekness and majesty,
manhood and deity,
in perfect harmony,
the man who is God:
Lord of eternity
dwells in humanity,
kneels in humility
and washes our feet.

Father's pure radiance,
perfect in innocence,
yet learns obedience
to death on a cross:
suffering to give us life,
conquering through sacrifice;
and, as they crucify,
prays "Father, forgive."

Wisdom unsearchable,
God the invisible,
Love indestructible
in frailty appears.
Lord of infinity,
stooping so tenderly,
lifts our humanity
to the heights of His throne.

Oh, what a mystery,
meekness and majesty:
bow down and worship,
for this is your God,
this is your God!

CHAPTER NINE

He works in ... we work out

What a chapter it has been so far, we have an impassioned appeal for unity, an example of an early Christian hymn or poem, a noble declaration on the Lordship of Jesus Christ, a profound illustration of unsurpassed excellence on the person and work of Jesus; all in the space of eleven verses and the end is not yet!

Paul has been showing us that the road to *happiness* is one where there is a real sense of unity in the family of God. As believers we are to engage our hearts in the pursuit of *humility* by following in the footsteps of Jesus when He became a servant. The end of that journey will take us to a place of *honour* when God will exalt us in His own good time. Now, he reminds us in verses 12-18 that the great goal in the life of the Christian should be that of *holiness*.

In the previous section we saw the pre-eminence of Christ. He is supreme in life, in death, in resurrection and now in glory. He is unique and He stands head and shoulders above all His would-be rivals. None can be seriously compared to Him. There is no real pretender waiting in the wings to take His throne. Having said that, the apostle leaves us in no doubt, that it is our salient responsibility to have an attitude akin to His. He has been describing for us the mind of Christ. Presently he would direct our interest to the dynamics of that same mind.

Yes, we read about it, we agree with it, we nod our heads in approval, we admire with spellbound eyes the example of Jesus, we are inspired by all that He has done, but, how do we get it? That's when the crunch comes!

He is the Pattern we would wish to copy. But, He is more. He also provides us with the power to make sure it becomes a reality in our lives. He will equip and enable us by His Spirit, He gives us not only the ability to keep our heads above the water but also to swim freely in the water. As Warren Wiersbe explains: "It is not by imitation, but by incarnation" that we are able to share the secrets of the mind of Christ. He did it! With His help, so can we!

We will discover that the Christian life is not a series of "ups and downs" but an ongoing process of "ins and outs." That means, God works *in*, and we work *out*.

ACHIEVING THE PURPOSE

The opening word, *"therefore"* (2:12), is the unavoidable connecting word between what has gone before and what is following after. It is a link with all that has been said and what he is about to say. The two are intertwined. One follows hard on the heels of the other. You say, Jesus is my reason for living; well, says Paul, here He is your recipe for life. You have seen the example, the way to do it; now, put it into practice, go and do it! Christ was obedient in death; they (and we) must be obedient in life.

It is imperative we remember Paul is writing here to those who are already members of God's family. That's why he calls them *"my dear friends"* (2:12). These words have nothing to do with his readers becoming Christians, they already are!

So, what are they to do?

Work out!

"continue to work out your salvation with fear and trembling" (2:12)

They were not to work for their own salvation, that is a gift from God! But, they were to work at it! If you like, they were to stop playing church and be zealously committed to the cause of Christ. They were to be sold out to Jesus. It was a stirring challenge to them to live out their faith and impact their community for Christ. He was exhorting them to get up out of their soft grandstand seats and get down to the pitch where the action was. The brand of Christianity being advocated by Paul is that of getting your feet wet. God is not looking for smooth clean hands but for dirty hands. That's work!

The phrase *"work out"* has the meaning of working something through to its full completion such as you would do when solving a mathematical problem. It was also used to describe those who worked in the mines in Paul's day, they would work it so as to reclaim the maximum amount that was possible. The term would also have been used in the context of farming, the farmer would work a field so as to secure the greatest harvest possible. It's all about realising the potential that is there. And, being serious in our quest for such a benefit.

Paul was saying to his friends at Philippi: "You have been given an incredible stockpile of resources, now go out and realise the full potential of all that you are and have in Jesus Christ."

He longs that we might lead fulfilled lives and that we might be at our best for God. He desires nothing more than we should maintain our spiritual glow and be at our peak for Him. He's looking for followers who will be spiritual fitness fanatics, that means we will have to fight the spiritual flab. Yes, discipline is vital and essential. There are no shortcuts. There is no easy course to adopt, it's a matter of working at it and working it out! A daily workout producing pints of spiritual sweat will ensure a leaner and fitter Christian.

Shine bright!

"Do everything without complaining or arguing, so that you may become blameless and pure, children of God without fault in a crooked and depraved generation, in which you shine like stars in the universe" (2:14,15)

The light always shines brightest where and when it is darkest. Today's world is inky black, our society is muddy and murky. Hence the need of the hour is for us to give careful heed to what Paul is saying in the above verses, and again, it is back to our attitude.

We are to watch our attitude. If we don't, it will manifest itself in two ways: complaining and arguing. The former is something we tend to do when we are alone, we grumble, we complain, we moan, we find fault.

We mutter under our breath and whine and whinge about anything and everything. It is totally negative. The latter is a characteristic that more often than not happens when we are with others. It is vocal and verbal abuse, it is open warfare on other people's character and ministry, it is making a song and dance about everything under the sun and doing it in such a way so as to stir up feelings of distrust and suspicion.

When you put the two of them together it can cause verbal pollution of such magnitude that it will take a heavy toll on everyone. The atmosphere is poisoned and lives are ruined because of acid rain comments.

Don't allow yourself to have an argumentative spirit, it only divides. Don't specialise in causing friction, it only disrupts the family. Don't sow seeds of discontent, it only discredits the name of Jesus.

Alright, we get the message, Paul; but, please be positive. What should we be like?

We should be distinctively different from the non Christian. We won't need to pontificate from our soap box or stand and shout it from the rooftop as it will be glaringly obvious to all with eyes to see that we wear our Christianity on our shirt sleeve.

To live a life that is *"blameless"* is to live with integrity so that no one can point an accusing finger. It is putting the purity back into everyday living. Another quality Paul would expect to find in our lives is that of being *"pure."* The thought here is of that which is unmixed and unadulterated. It is the picture of innocence, someone who is inexperienced in evil and untainted in motive. It is staying clean in a corrupt society. It is walking through the coal mine of this world without getting dirty. To be *"without fault"* is to be free of defect or blemish and is a word that finds its origin in the sacrificial lambs that were destined for the altar. It is to be above and beyond reproach.

The standards are high. They have got to be. In a world where anything goes we should be men and women who will stand out in a crowd. It's a call to cheerful living in a world oozing with unhappiness. And, it's a clarion call to walk straight in a society that is warped and crooked. Men today are so twisted they could hide behind a corkscrew, that's why we should be walking tall with our heads held high for Jesus. In a community that is riddled with so much that is foul and filthy we ought to be shining as luminaries for the Lord.

Hold out!

"hold out the word of life" (2:16)

We are to seize every opportunity that is afforded to us to share the Word of life with others. In a world that is decadent, dark and dead it is the Word alone that can bring about a lasting change. Because it is known as the Word of life it implies there is life in the Word. And there is!

We need to hold it fast, that's the defensive position. We need to hold it forth, that's the offensive stance.

The phrase that Paul employed to describe this act is most vivid and graphic. It paints the picture of a host offering a refreshing drink to a guest at a banquet or celebration. That's what the gospel entails, it represents the gracious offer of the gospel of Jesus Christ to those who do not know Him.

What a challenge to each of us. There's the purpose that needs to be achieved. We can't stop the world and get off. We would be foolish to adopt the ostrich mentality and bury our head in the sand and pretend it's not as bad as they say it is. We dare not risk becoming spiritual hermits and living in isolation. We can't opt out or cop out! We're here! And, because of what our Lord Jesus did, we owe it to Him to work it out in our present environment.

RECEIVING THE POWER

"for it is God who works in you to will and to act according to His good purpose" (2:13)

This is marvellous because it tells me that God is actively working in us. The principle is as old as the hills. I think of Moses whose dream to be a leader in Egypt was smashed when he identified with his own people and killed an Egyptian. Banished to Midian, he became a shepherd; the very occupation was loathsome to the Egyptians (Genesis 46:34). Surely this was a source of frustration to him. He had been trained in hieroglyphics, chemistry, mathematics, and astronomy, and now he had to set all of these skills aside and do what he had been taught was detestable. Talk about someone who was over-qualified for his position!

Yet Moses learned, as all of us must, that there are some lessons that cannot be learned in a palace, but must be learned in a desert. He spent 40 years in the desert looking after a flock of sheep before God used him to lead the fledgling nation of Israel out of the land of Egypt. Those were days of preparation when God was moulding and shaping the life of His servant. This is Philippians 2:13 in action.

You see, God is more interested in the man than He is in the ministry. He is more concerned about the workman than He is about the work. That is the main reason why He chooses to work in us before operating through us.

Why do we obey Him? It should not be in response to pressure from the outside but from a power on the inside.

It is *"God ... in you"* - there we have the entrance of God into our lives. Why does He bother doing it? It is *"according to His good purpose"* - that reminds me of His enjoyment. How does He accomplish it? It is because He *"works in you"* - surely that indicates the energy of God.

There are two little phrases of two words each that are used to describe what God does, *"to will"* and *"to act."* Both the desire and the deed belong to God. Both the prompting and the performing are attributed to Him.

We're almost back to where we started, He works in and we work out. It is a joint initiative, a partnership. It is a shared programme of activity. We respond to what He has done. I chuckled when I came across a story that illustrates this truth rather well. It is the tale of a country farmer who was visited by his new fresh faced pastor. As the pastor surveyed the farm for the first time, he commented, "John, this is a great farm you and God have!" "Thank you," said John. "But you should have been here five years ago and seen it when God had it all by Himself!" Only a story, maybe. But the lesson is clear. God works through us. He will not do for us what we should be doing for ourselves. As we cooperate with Him we can see the potential of our lives being realised.

BELIEVING THE PROMISE

"... in order that I may boast on the day of Christ that I did not run or labour for nothing. But even if I am being poured out like a drink offering on the sacrifice and service coming from your faith, I am glad and rejoice with all of you. So you too should be glad and rejoice with me" (2:16-18)

There is a double sense of joy in the verses just quoted:

A joy in the there and then

He is speaking about the day of Christ. That is the same moment he spoke of previously in 1:6 as the day of accountability. He lived his life in the light of the judgment seat of Christ. He performed his service with eternity written upon his heart and soul. He lived today in the light of tomorrow. Today he was with them, tomorrow he may be with Him. And, he did not want to be ashamed or embarrassed. He longed that his life's work might redound to His glory. As he looked back over many years he wanted to be able to do it with a sense of real satisfaction and pleasure. That brought joy!

A joy in the here and now

This finds its focus in sacrifice and service, strange bedfellows to produce joy, you may be tempted to think. But no. He is simply walking down the same road that Jesus walked before him. He sees himself as a drink offering, he has poured out his life and his love on the altar for Jesus. And for them. As he emptied himself so God filled him to overflowing with a joy that was outrageous, he was a man saturated with God.

It's a matter of striking a balance. If we want to maintain a spiritual equilibrium we will need to realise that God works in, and, we work out. Then, and only then, we will find as Warren Wiersbe says, "life is not a series of disappointing ups and downs. Rather, it is a sequence of delightful ins and outs."

CHAPTER TEN

Great minds think alike

There's a story of a repair man who crawled high up into the steeple of a church early one morning to investigate a problem with the ventilation system. To his chagrin he slipped, and as he began to fall, he grabbed the rope that was connected to the church bell. Needless to say, he woke up the whole town!

Sometimes life is like that. You find out that even ordinary experiences have repercussions far beyond what anyone could ever imagine. A small event can have big consequences. Recall that World War 1 began when the Archduke Franz Ferdinand, heir to the throne of Austria-Hungary, and his wife Sophie were assassinated! The death of two people set in motion the death of millions.

Similarly, a small act of kindness can have unpredictably beneficial consequences. Edward Kimball certainly had no idea that one of the boys in his Sunday School class, who had such difficulty understanding the Gospel, would eventually shake two continents for God. Despite his obscure beginnings as a shoe salesman, D. L. Moody went on to become one of the world's greatest evangelists and his legacy continues.

That's exactly what happened to the apostle Paul.

You will remember in Acts 14:6,7 Paul is on his first missionary journey and he finds himself in the cities of Lystra and Derbe. He and Barnabas are preaching their hearts out when the unthinkable happens.

A miracle takes place and within minutes the crowd are convinced that they have come from another planet, *"the gods have come down to us in human form!"* He tried unsuccessfully to convince the people that they were human just like them, they even tore their shirts off their backs in an attempt to reveal their plain vanilla humanity! It didn't work. It wasn't very long until rent-a-mob had gathered from another town and began to stone Paul and Barnabas. He was dragged outside the city and left for dead. The next day they moved on to Derbe where a mighty work of grace took place in that they *"won a large number of disciples."*

It was in either Lystra or Derbe, amid all the mayhem and miracles, that Paul bumped into Timothy in the "enquiry room." He listened to the young man's story. He heard about his parents. His mother was of Jewish origin and was called Eunice; and, his father whose name is unknown was of Greek extraction. It would appear that Timothy's childhood upbringing was more strongly influenced by his father because he was not circumcised until he was a young adult. Having said that, it is obvious that his maternal grandmother, Lois, played a leading role in his life. Together with his mother they sought to give him a good grounding in the things of the Lord (cf. 2 Timothy 1:5 and 3:14,15). Both of them were godly ladies. There must have been something beautiful and attractive about their witness as when Paul arrived on the scene young Timothy was quick to respond to the good news of Jesus. He was handpicked fruit, ripe and ready to be plucked for the Lord.

We have no way of knowing how long Paul spent counselling Timothy on that memorable day, it may have been 20 or 25 minutes, who could have anticipated the outcome of that conversation? Who ever would have thought then that a short time later Paul would return to this same area on his second missionary journey and invite Timothy to join him? Fantastic, isn't it! Read all about it in Acts 16:1-3.

This heralded the start of a lifelong friendship when Timothy proved to be worth more than his weight in gold. They laughed together. They cried together. They preached together. They travelled together. There was nothing forced about their relationship, it just flowed naturally. It was all so easy looking and enormously rewarding. In fact, it was such a high profile partnership that Timothy is mentioned twenty-four times in Paul's letters and is identified with Paul in the writing of five letters.

And, after many years of fruitful service together, when the older man was promoted to glory, his successor was Timothy (cf. 2 Timothy 4:1-11). He had been groomed for such a role and was ready to fill it when occasion deemed that it was right. That was wise planning on Paul's part and a worthwhile investment of his expertise in the life of another individual. This is classic text book material being put into practice on basic discipleship.

TIMOTHY: You're the man to go

You can see the way Paul's mind works, he is extremely well organised and seems to have no hangups about delegating responsibility. He is fairly relaxed when it comes to telling other people what to do and where to go. It is clear from his epistle that he is happy to block out a few days in another man's diary so that he can receive an up to the minute report on life in Philippi. We read: *"I hope in the Lord Jesus to send Timothy to you soon, that I also may be cheered when I receive news about you"* (2:19).

When D + J = P + T

The obvious man for the job was Timothy! He flatly confesses that he *"has no-one else like him"* (2:20), they have a kindred spirit. It's all about great minds thinking alike! They were on the same wavelength, or as Charles Swindoll comments, "... they thought alike. Their perspectives were in line with each other. Timothy would interpret situations much like Paul, had the latter been there. When the older sent the younger on a fact-finding mission he could rely on the report as being similar to one he himself would have brought back." There was a oneness of spirit between the two of them. I would imagine that it was not unlike the closeness David enjoyed with Jonathan (cf. 1 Samuel 18:1;20:17). There was a unique and unusual depth in their understanding of each other, neither would have to speak because the one knew what the other was thinking!

TIMOTHY: You're the man who cares

Paul can't speak highly enough of young Timothy, he reminds the Christians in Philippi that Timothy *"takes a genuine interest in their wel-*

fare" (2:20). He loved people. He cared for people. He was concerned about the needs of others. He wanted to do all he could to alleviate their suffering, he had a heart for people. Paul had no reservations lurking in the front of his mind about his choice of envoy. He knew Timothy would be able to handle the people well without adding to the tension they were experiencing. He could rest easy because Timothy would provide an answer rather than adding to their problems.

TIMOTHY: You're the ONLY man who cares

"For everyone looks out for his own interests, not those of Jesus Christ" (2:21)

Can you imagine it? There were hundreds of Christians in the city of Rome, yet not one was available to make this trip across to Philippi. Paul couldn't find one! The reason: they were too busy doing their own thing to worry about anyone else. They were immersed in themselves and couldn't see any further than their own nose. If it wasn't in their backyard they showed an appalling lack of interest. They were totally wrapped up in their own affairs.

It doesn't say much for their spirituality. It says a lot about their lack of consecration and commitment to the body of Christ. They needed to sort themselves out when it came to assessing priorities; in a very real sense, all of us live either in Philippians 1:21 or Philippians 2:21!

TIMOTHY: You've served your time well

Paul has a wonderful way with words as he quietly reassures the church at Philippi as to Timothy's suitability for the job in hand. It's the power of positive thinking as he says, *"but you know that Timothy has proved himself, because as a son with his father he has served with me in the work of the gospel"* (2:22).

He has served his apprenticeship well, he has come through every test with flying colours, he is a man of calibre. He is quality personified. He has character. Paul wasn't the only one who spoke in such glowing language of this young man. Remember the statement recorded in Acts 16:2 by the leaders of his local church: *"the brothers at Lystra and Iconium spoke well of him."*

Paul gave him lots of practical experience in various situations so that he would develop an all round ministry. His was on the job in-house training and it proved to be more than satisfactory. What a privilege it was for Timothy to learn from the greatest exponent in the early church on how-to and how-not-to do it.

ENTER EPAPHRODITUS

There is a subtle difference in how Paul deals with Timothy and Epaphroditus. Because of the relationship they enjoyed, Paul wrote of who Timothy was. But when he mentions this second gentleman, Epaphroditus, he puts his finger on what he did. Timothy is a marvellous example of service and Epaphroditus is a superb model of suffering.

He was a highly respected member of the church at Philippi and had been commissioned by them to take a monetary gift to Paul and to stay with him as long as possible during his confinement in Rome. He was a man whom they could trust implicitly with such an important assignment.

He hadn't been in Rome very long when he developed a serious life threatening illness. He almost died. Eventually, however, he made a complete recovery. In between times, as is often the case, word filtered back to the church via the bush telegraph and they were understandably perplexed and perturbed about his rumoured condition. To make matters worse, he was worrying about them worrying about him!

When the dust had settled, Paul felt it would be prudent to send Epaphroditus back home so that the folks there would see how miraculously he had been restored to health. Paul was at pains to point out in the course of his comments that Epaphroditus had been a tremendous blessing to him and he was standing by him with unswerving loyalty, there may have been some gossip and criticism among the members about him coming back as a quitter or even about him being the best choice in the first place. Paul quickly extinguished the smouldering embers of idle chit-chat. And, so as to kill two birds with one stone, Paul sent this letter back with him! That was how they received the epistle to the Philippians ...

Meet Mr Charming

Yes, believe it or not, but that is what his name means. He lived up to his name. If you could meet him you would not be disappointed, he was a lovely man. One writer says of him, "Apart from these few verses he would be an unknown, but in many respects, that fits him anyway. He was just a layman in the church at Philippi who held no office, wrote no books, gave no sermons, led no great enterprises for God. He was a messenger boy for the gospel, a servant for his Lord. No task was too menial for him to do. No assignment was too little for him to accept. No risk was too great for him to take. He would have been comfortable with a towel and basin."

He's a Jack of all trades

Paul clearly thought the sun rose and set on Epaphroditus. He counted him and valued him as a dear friend. He described him in 2:25 as:

"my brother" - they were bound by a common love because they were united as brothers in the same spiritual family. There was a warmth in their Christian experience. This is further elaborated on by Paul when you see his immense relief that Epaphroditus has been spared (cf. 2:27b).

"fellow-worker" - they were both involved in the service of the Lord and were keen to see the gospel triumph in the hearts of men and women, boys and girls. He had an entrepreneurial spirit like Paul as they shared together in the ministry of the Word of God.

"fellow-soldier" - it is never enough to be just a worker in the ministry. One must also learn as he did to be a warrior. Facing danger has an unusual way of bonding lives together as men learn to depend on each other. There were many open doors but there were also many adversaries. It was a battle.

He joined the Parabolani

Never heard of them? Let me fill you in on the details. It's too good to miss. We read in 2:30 that Epaphroditus *"risked his life"* in order to minister effectively into the situation that Paul found himself in. It has the idea of someone hazarding their life for someone else, they would gamble against the odds, the stakes might be high but they would be willing to take the risk. If there was even a slim chance of success they would put their money where their mouth was, it's the betting man's way of looking at life. Those people became known as the parabolani or the riskers! And, our friend, Epaphroditus along with the likes of Aquila and Priscilla (cf. Romans 16:3,4) were paid up members of this elite club.

He's a hero

Paul says, *"welcome him in the Lord with great joy, and honour men like him, because he almost died for the work of Christ"* (2:29,30). He deserves a hero's welcome when he returns home. It should be an occasion for throwing a party in his honour, it is an excuse for a celebration and deservedly so. Men who are willing to do what Epaphroditus did are few and far between and so they should be respected and revered. These are men who dice with death and don't stop to ask questions. They flirt openly with death and do it out of a sense of loyalty to their friends and love for their Lord. These men are one in a million. Says Paul, thank God for them!

When you look at them, Paul, Timothy and Epaphroditus, they are as different as day and night. Forget about Paul for a moment. Here were two very ordinary men, two special friends of Paul, two companions who lived in the shadow of the great man, two men from nowhere who were going somewhere; one of them, Timothy, we hear and read a lot about; the other one, Epaphroditus, he appears and before you get your tongue round the pronunciation of his name, he has gone. He's only mentioned twice in Paul's letters!

Take the two of them together, Timothy and Epaphroditus, they were ready to be sent anywhere, they were ready to serve anyone, and they were ready to sacrifice anything. Add Paul and the three of them are a formidable trio of great minds thinking alike!

CHAPTER ELEVEN

The reality of being a Christian

Have you heard the latest definition of an optimist?

An optimist is a person who believes the preacher is almost finished when he says *"finally."*

Did you see the opening word in chapter 3 of Paul's little letter to a small band of believers living in ancient Philippi? You've guessed it! It's the word, *"finally."*

An interesting statistic is that in chapters 1 and 2 there is a total of 60 verses. When you count up the total in chapters 3 and 4 you have another 44 verses, and he says, *"finally."* He really can't be serious! And, to further confuse the issue, he's only starting the second half of his epistle according to the chapter divisions. Makes you think, doesn't it?

So, what does Paul mean when he says, *"finally?"* It's almost like a change of gear as he moves into overdrive. He keeps on going and he has no intention of applying the brakes just yet. He has not used the word in a conclusive sense, it could read like this: *"as for the rest, my brothers ..."* (3:1).

REJOICE! REJOICE! REJOICE!

If they didn't get the message the first time, he was determined they would get it this time. That's why he says, *"rejoice in the Lord"* (3:1). This is the underlying theme of his letter and he wants to underscore the importance of them being a people whose lives are categorised as joyful. How vital that is!

Our happiness depends on happenings but even when things begin to go wrong we can still have joy. His joy is such that circumstances cannot even change it. It is immune to the highs and lows of everyday life, it is not influenced by the emotional seesaw we sometimes are sitting on. Our circumstances may be less than conducive, our present situation may cause us considerable concern and be a source of nagging worry to our minds, the forecast may seem rather ominous, and in such moments we don't feel like rejoicing. But we can! This joy is not artificial. It is not a thin veneer of superficial smiles. It is fixed and rooted in the Lord. We may not be able to rejoice in our circumstances, but we can still rejoice in the Lord (cf. Habakkuk 3:17,18).

The apostle is really setting the tone for the rest of the chapter. They were not to rejoice in who they were and what they had done. They were to rejoice in Jesus Christ and all that He had done.

Paul makes no apology for going back over old ground. He believes that repetition is the mother of all learning, if you say something often enough people will eventually allow it to sink in and they will slowly come round to believing it. Hence his comment, *"it is no trouble for me to write the same things to you again, and it is a safeguard for you"* (3:1). He never grew tired or weary of telling them to enjoy the blessings God had given to them in the Lord Jesus. And, so far as Paul is concerned, joy should be near the top of the list.

THE ALARM BELLS ARE RINGING

Paul's language is less than complimentary when he sees what is happening in Philippi. There is a hint of realistic sarcasm in the tone of his voice as he labels false teachers for what they really are. He says, *"watch out"* (3:2). They were to be on red alert as the enemy was alive and well in their community. It is a challenge to them to be constantly on guard and to be looking over their shoulder as well as looking ahead. They have been warned!

I suppose the tendency is for us to become so comfortable, so complacent, so cushioned in our Christianity that before we know it carelessness has swept like an unassailable tidal wave into our lives. We are maybe not as vigilant as we ought to be or as conscious of the enemy's tactics as we should be. He says, beware!

A TRIPLE WARNING

This is strong language, he is bold and blunt, he brands them: "*... dogs, men who do evil ... mutilators of the flesh*" (3:2). He's not talking about three different groups of people. He is describing the same group in three different ways. He is referring to the Judaisers whose religion was a mixture of law and grace.

When he refers to them as *"dogs"*, Paul doesn't have in mind the family pet that we pamper and play with. It's not the "pedigree chum" kind of dog with a Cruft's medal hanging around its neck. No, certainly not! He's talking about people, in his day the orthodox Jew would call a Gentile a dog, here Paul refers to them as dogs. They are Christians of the canine variety!

Paul is not in the business of slinging mud at people. Nor is he calling names. He is, however, comparing these false teachers to dirty disease carrying scavengers who are potentially dangerous. They will snap at your heels. They will bark out their erroneous doctrine. They pose a menacing threat to anyone who is unsuspecting. They were troublemakers.

He speaks of them as *"men who do evil."* Jesus would have referred to them as "wolves in sheep's clothing." These are the people who wriggle and worm their way into a congregation and teach that a sinner is saved by faith plus good works. They are legalists. It has been said of them that "their message is full of exhortations to do more, to work harder, to witness longer, to pray with greater intensity, because enough is never enough."

Oh yes, they may sing the songs, they may use the language of Zion; they are the grey pin-striped suit brigade, the smooth talker, the well heeled, the effervescent personality. Paul says, beware of them as they peddle their wares. Don't be fooled!

An interesting turn of phrase is applied to them when he calls them *"mutilators of the flesh."* The word "mutilation" refers to the cutting of circumcision. In other words, when these false teachers required the young believers to be circumcised in order to be saved, they were guilty of mutilating the flesh of these brethren. Their confidence was in the flesh.

The fact of the matter is that the true Christian has experienced a spiritual circumcision in Christ, he does not need any fleshly operation. These men invite you to come to Christ with the Bible in one hand and a sharp surgical knife in the other!

You can understand why Paul was so hard on these men. They posed a very real threat to the people of God in the first century. He knows if you give them an inch they will take more than the customary mile. Don't be hoodwinked! Don't be caught napping! Don't be conned, they are only a bunch of spiritual crooks. They're guilty of spiritual piracy.

TWO MILLENNIA LATER

The problem is as real at the end of the twentieth century and the challenge from Paul is just as relevant. Lewis Johnson has unmasked the villain in his remarkable expose when he concludes: "One of the most serious problems facing the orthodox Christian church today is the problem of legalism. One of the most serious problems facing the church in Paul's day was the problem of legalism. In every day it is the same. Legalism wrenches the joy of the Lord from the Christian believer, and with the joy of the Lord goes his power for vital worship and vibrant witness. Nothing is left but cramped, sombre, dull, and listless profession. The truth is betrayed, and the glorious name of the Lord becomes a synonym for a gloomy kill-joy. The Christian under the law is a miserable parody of the real thing."

WORSHIP AS IT WAS MEANT TO BE

Paul communicates the simple truth to his friends in Philippi when he shows the remarkable difference between them and the false teachers. It's a them and us situation. They glory in who they are and in what they are, we glory in the Person and work of our Lord Jesus. Says Paul, *"we are the circumcision"* (3:3), what a daring statement to make! Our salvation is not something outward, it is a deep inner work of the

Holy Spirit in the life of the child of God. It is not found in some religious ritual or ceremony, it lies exclusively in the finished work of Christ on Calvary. It's not for the body, it's a matter for the heart.

How do we show it?

by responding to God in the Spirit

Paul reminds us that we are those *"who worship by the Spirit of God"* (3:3). True worship is conducted in the human heart in the power of the Holy Spirit. This finds an echo in the sentiments of Jesus recorded in John 4:24 and is also indicative of the desire expressed by David in Psalm 24:4. When we are occupied with Him, when we become taken in with Him, when He becomes central in our love and devotion, this can only happen by the Spirit within.

by rejoicing in Christ Jesus alone

Paul takes his argument a step further when he describes us as those *"who glory in Christ Jesus"* (3:3). The Christian will find his joy in the Lord Jesus, He becomes number one in our lives, He is Lord of all. He alone is worthy. In ourselves we have nothing to commend us, left to go our own way we would be lost, when the heart is captivated by Him then all the praise is ascribed to Him. He gets all the glory. And, rightly so!

by refusing to trust in the flesh

Paul declares we *"put no confidence in the flesh"* (3:3). There is nothing we can do in our old nature to win His smile of approval. There is no good in any of us that would merit a place in heaven. The old man has nothing going for it, it wars against the spiritual new nature. Oh, I can't do it, but He can! Our dependence is upon Him. He is the Rock on which we stand. What a relief. God's grace has again come to our rescue. And in the process He gets the glory. All the credit goes to Him, as certainly it should.

Charles Swindoll feels that when Paul was writing such words "he must have experienced a flashback to the way he was for so many years - in fact, all of his adult life. Before his conversion, he was the personification of a proud Pharisee. Nobody's trophy case was larger. Had they given an award for high achievement in the field of religion, Paul would have won top honours in his nation year after year. His wall could have been covered with plaques, diplomas, framed letters from influential individuals, and numerous artifacts - all impressive."

He looked at them and he looked at himself in his former days and there's no match. They were in a different league to him, he was in the premier league and they were languishing in the lower divisions. They would have a lot of ground to make up if they were going to catch up with Paul, a virtual impossibility. He was the king of the castle, they were left standing outside in the cold as also-rans. Therein lies the significance behind his reasoning when he says, *"if anyone else thinks he has reasons to put confidence in the flesh, I have more"* (3:4). He has the credentials to prove it. He has the record to back up all that he says about himself, make no mistake about it, he was a high flyer!

THE C.V. OF A HIGH ACHIEVER

Paul gives us his pedigree in the following verses by going back to his roots. It's an autobiographical sketch when Paul traces his heritage and records his many outstanding achievements. He outstripped his contemporaries and eclipsed all other lights. He was a giant among pygmies, in comparison to him they suffered from a grasshopper complex.

Look at what he says about himself: I was *"circumcised on the eighth day, of the people of Israel, of the tribe of Benjamin, a Hebrew of Hebrews; in regard to the law, a Pharisee; as for zeal, persecuting the church; as for legalistic righteousness, faultless"* (3:5,6).

William Barclay in his book *The Mind of St. Paul* explains the thinking behind each of these seven assets listed by Paul. He says, "If ever there was a Jew who was steeped in Judaism, that Jew was Paul. Let us ... look again at the claims he had to be the Jew *par excellence*. He was circumcised on the eighth day; that is to say, he bore in the body the badge and the mark that he was one of the chosen people, marked out by God as His own. He was of the race of Israel; that is to say, he was a member of the nation who stood in a covenant relationship with God, a relationship in which no other people stood. He was of the tribe of Benjamin. This is a claim which Paul reiterates in Romans 11:1. What is the point of this claim? The tribe of Benjamin had a unique place in the history of Israel. It was from Benjamin that the first king of Israel had come, for Saul was a Benjamite ... Benjamin was the only one of the patriarchs who had actually been born in the land of promise. When Israel went into battle, it was the tribe of Benjamin which held the post of honour. The battle cry of Israel was: 'After thee, O Benjamin' ...

In lineage Paul was not only an Israelite; he was of the aristocracy of Israel. He was a Hebrew of the Hebrews; that is to say, Paul was not one of these Jews of the Dispersion who, in a foreign land, had forgotten their own tongue; he was a Jew who still remembered and knew the language of his fathers.

He was a Pharisee; that is to say, he was not only a devout Jew; he was more - he was one of 'The Separated Ones' who had foresworn all normal activities in order to dedicate life to the keeping of the Law, and he had kept it with such meticulous care that in the keeping of it he was blameless ...

Paul knew Judaism at its best and at its highest; he knew it from the inside; he had gone through all the experiences, both of height and of depth that it could bring to any man."

What a man! What earnest endeavour! What qualifications! He could boast in his ancestry. He could boast in his orthodoxy. What he did backed up all he believed. There was no contradiction between his belief and behaviour, he was without blame. No man could justifiably point an accusing finger at him. He had it made! He made it! Not really, when he opens up the books to see what wealth he has, he discovers he is bankrupt!

The radical difference came about when he met Jesus on the Damascus Road. He quickly discovered that all of the achievements he had under his belt meant nothing in the light of the righteousness of Christ. All that he had attained and worked hard for faded into oblivion when weighed in the scales of divine justice. By the world's tape measure, Paul's success was staggering. But by God's standards, it didn't amount to much.

Standing before Jesus Christ, blinded by a heavenly light, he was humbled, for the first time in his life. He realised he had nothing to offer as he was stripped of all his assets, and he knew that he was a nobody! It only took a moment spent in the presence of the Lord of glory for him to realise that he had spent his entire life on the wrong road travelling towards the wrong destination for all the wrong reasons.

It was *"nothing in my hands I bring, simply to Thy cross I cling,"* it was that time for Paul. It was make up your mind time, this was his hour of decision. And, thank God, he didn't flinch from making the wise choice.

When Jesus Christ invaded the life of Saul of Tarsus He performed a creative act. It was a miracle of metamorphosis, an inside-out transformation. Just as a caterpillar's whole body dissolves in the cocoon and is restructured into a beautiful butterfly, so our entire being dissolves and is given a new life in the Lord Jesus Christ. He became a brand new creation.

He was reconciled. He was given a transfusion of joy. He was forgiven. He was accepted into the global family of God. He had religion, now he has found reality. That's why he says: *"rejoice in the Lord."*

CHAPTER TWELVE

Taking a spiritual inventory

The story is told of the little boy who fell out of bed ... when his mum asked him what happened, he said: "I stayed too near where I got in."

We smile. But it wasn't us who landed on the floor! Nevertheless, that's how it is with so many of the Lord's people today. They have stayed too near where they got in. That could never be said of the apostle Paul. He was always on the move crossing new frontiers for the gospel. He was stepping out where man had never been before with the story of redemption. But it wasn't always like that.

He and David had one common trait, both could say: *"the boundary lines have fallen for me in pleasant places; surely I have a delightful inheritance"* (Psalm 16:6). Yes, he had a heritage to be proud of! He was an intellectual genius. He had successfully climbed the social ladder. His was the name dropped by everybody who was anybody. He had made it to the top. From a human point of view, he was born with a golden spoon in his mouth. Then, out of the blue, something happened that was to radically alter the course of his life. He would never be the same again.

I WAS THERE WHEN IT HAPPENED

He met Jesus! What an encounter it proved to be. Life-changing. He was turned around on the road of life to face a new direction. He was turned inside out and given a new outlook and perspective on life. God stopped him in the suburbs of Damascus and called a halt to his maddening pace, he was going fast nowhere. And, when the Saviour laid hold of him, his whole life was altered. Needless to say, this was when he really started to live.

It is nothing short of sensational, it's the kind of front page story the local supermarket press would have a field day with. You could just imagine the bold headlines emblazoned across the tabloids of his day! The *Daily Whatever-you-want-to-call-it* would not hesitate to capitalise on such a scoop. They would make a fortune from it! The tills would be ringing as it's the kind of story that sells newspapers.

THERE'S MORE TO LIFE THAN ...

"But whatever was to my profit I now consider loss for the sake of Christ" (3:7)

In the previous chapter we looked closely at Paul's list of achievements as detailed in verses 5 and 6. Then it happened. That's why he says *"but."* He has now been given a new frame of reference, everything has changed. Yes, he is discovering that there is more to life than ... all he had before! His values were reversed. These are not the words of a modest man; these are the gripping words of a transformed man, transformed by Jesus Christ.

In this particular verse Paul is sitting down at the desk with the book of his life open before him. He is totting up the figures. He looked at the credit entries and the debit entries. When he had finished *"considering"* or "counting" he produced a profit and loss account.

He is taking stock of his position. He is making a spiritual inventory so that he can accurately assess where he is at. And when he looks at the computer printout it's fairly obvious what has happened, the whole picture has altered because of one transaction.

In one column there was his impeccable pedigree, his outstanding past, his fantastic achievements, his personal portfolio, his impressive array of qualifications, all gains. See what has taken place. Every single entry has moved from the asset column to the liability column. He has nothing!

In the other column only one entry is recorded, conversion to Christ.

Now, he has everything!

WHEN GAIN IS LOSS AND LOSS IS GAIN

When Paul speaks of his deficit total he used the word *"loss"* which is only found in one other place in the New Testament. Ironically, it is mentioned in Acts 27:10,21 where it describes the loss and damage suffered by the ship on which Paul was taken as a prisoner to Rome. It is a "real life" illustration of how that which is gain can become loss. The ship which was bound for Italy had cargo aboard which was meant to bring considerable gain to its owner. If the crew had not thrown it overboard, all of the passengers on board could have been casualties. The cargo was jettisoned and the ship ran aground breaking its back, but the passengers and the crew were saved (see Acts 27:38-41).

Everything that was to be gain became loss so that the lives of men and women might be saved. Similarly, with the apostle Paul, all the "cargo" of his past life had to be thrown overboard so that he might gain his own spiritual life in Jesus Christ.

Jim Eliot hit the nail on the head when he penned in his diary: "He is no fool who gives what he cannot keep to gain what he cannot lose."

MEANWHILE, THIRTY YEARS LATER

Three decades have come and gone. Has Paul? Let him speak for himself: *"What is more, I consider everything a loss compared to the surpassing greatness of knowing Christ Jesus my Lord, for whose sake I have lost all things. I consider them rubbish, that I may gain Christ and be found in Him, not having a righteousness of my own that comes from the law, but that which is through faith in Christ - the righteousness that comes from God and is by faith"* (3:8,9).

The passing of time has not diminished his zeal for the Lord nor has it dampened his enthusiasm in serving the greatest Master of all. A lot of water has gone under the bridge in thirty years but Paul is still aiming high in his quest for an intimate knowledge of Christ.

This is what he says after he has tried it, he has found it really works. Here is the voice of experience. He has no doubts in his mind. There is not even a tinge of disappointment. At the second count, he reckons there is nothing in this world that can be compared with the heart's pursuit of God. There's a thrill in knowing Jesus. It gives you a tingle that nothing else can. Getting to know God better has to be seen as the ultimate adventure.

It not only involves the mind of the Christian in that we apply ourselves to a serious study of the Word of God. As we acquaint ourselves with Him in the pages of Scripture so we familiarise ourselves with the great doctrines of grace and glory. We become avid readers of the sacred page and keen listeners to the preached Word.

It goes a few inches lower and captivates the affections of the heart. It all becomes so personal when we exclaim with Thomas: *"my Lord."*

THEY'RE FIT FOR THE TIP

When Paul analyses his present position in Christ he is overwhelmed. He is almost lost for words as he knows he is immeasurably better off. He has a richness in his life that money can't buy. His knowledge of God is worth more than acres of diamonds.

Everything else, says Paul, is worthless. It is *"rubbish."* It is fit for the tip. His past and all the glories associated with it are as good as trash and ideal consumption for dogs. In reality, they're of no more value than left-overs. That means, nothing! Garbish! Debris! Ideal for an incinerator.

HE LOST BUT HE'S NOT A LOSER

He lost his reputation and his religion but he gained far more than he lost. He's not a loser in either the short term or the long term. God never short changes His people. Paul is now *"found in Him"* and he couldn't be in a better place. There is no safer place on earth. Because of his relationship with the Lord he has also been made righteous. The righteousness of Christ has been imparted and imputed to him. This is not the "works righteousness" we read of in verse 6 but the "faith righteousness" that is talked about in verse 9. The former depends on the sinner; the latter depends on the Saviour. What happened was this: sin was transferred *from* his account and righteousness transferred *to* his account. That is God's system of book-keeping!

Charles Swindoll says, "at that epochal moment divine righteousness was credited to his empty account, and he saw himself reclothed in the imputed righteousness of Christ. That changed everything within him and about him."

No wonder Paul had a joy that was blissfully outrageous. He wasn't wrapped up in the trinkets of religion, he wasn't interested in all the holy hardware with all its trimmings and trappings any longer. For too many years he knew he was engrossed in a cheap religion, now he has reality. He has found to his immense personal pleasure that Christianity is Christ. He could sing with the song-writer: "He is my everything, He is my all!"

TO KNOW HIM AND MAKE HIM KNOWN

When Paul reached the point in his life of surrender to the Lord Jesus he edges forward in his desire to know God intimately. Paul has seen so many folks who were content to live their lives on the low road. That's not for him. He's taking the high road. The mediocre, humdrum, run-of-the-mill, ordinary life is not even entertained in his mind for a moment, he is a man who is jumping on the springboard in his attempt to reach higher heights with the Lord. Here is the heart cry of a man earnestly longing after God.

He says, "Lord, I want to know you better! Lord, I want to know you more and more!"

It took him a wee while to get there. It didn't happen overnight. There are no instant results when it comes to true spirituality. You can't snap your fingers and demand it as if you were waiting for a meal in a restaurant where the service was at a snail's pace. Someone has said, "Heaven never hangs out the sign: Overnight Transformations. Enquire Within."

Paul was a thinker, he was a man with a razor sharp mind; and, he was a theologian, he was a man with a warm heart. That didn't satisfy the cravings of the inner man. And so he sat down one day and reflected on his past life and prayerfully assessed his present experience, the conclusion he came to is echoed in his personal vision statement. This is how he wants to spend the rest of his life.

He says, *"I want to know Christ and the power of His resurrection and the fellowship of sharing in His sufferings, becoming like Him in His death, and so, somehow, to attain to the resurrection from the dead"* (3:10,11).

A Person worth knowing

This is one of Paul's continuing aims, *"to know Him."* It is a goal that he is determinedly seeking after. It is an all-consuming passion in his life. Yes, he came to know Him on the Damascus Road, that was alright for starters! He wants more than a casual acquaintance, more than a "oh yes, I recognise him" relationship. He's talking about that which is experiential.

It is not the *know* of the intellect but the *know* of intimacy.

We all know the Prime Minister of the United Kingdom; that is, we know his name, John Major, we know who he is; but very few of us know him personally. Most of us will be aware of the identity of the President of the United States, we know who he is, Bill Clinton; even fewer among us would claim to know him personally. That is the difference between knowing someone and *really* knowing someone!

In the idyllic setting of the Highlands and Islands of Scotland many of the crofters cottages had two rooms. They were called "a but" and "a ben." No matter who it was came to the front door they would be automatically shown into the but. There were some notable exceptions to that general rule, when a special friend called to visit they would be taken into the ben. There's a difference in the relationship but not in the warmth of the welcome. That is why you would often hear the crofters saying among themselves, rather quaintly: "I see you were far ben with so-and-so."

Paul is saying: "I want to be far ben with God!"

A power worth having

We have known the *"power of His resurrection"* in the past, because at the moment of our conversion, we were raised up with Christ and seated in heavenly places (cf. Ephesians 2:6). We can know that *"power"* in the present, for Christ's resurrection was accomplished so that we might *"live a new life"* (cf. Romans 6:4). We will know that *"power"* completely in the future when our bodies will be raised up just as His was (cf. 1 Corinthians 15).

Here is the dynamic of God in the life of the believer. It is like dynamite, something explosive. It has all the potential to blow the mind and it will enable us to maximise the potency of God in our lives. How we need to live our lives *"in the power of the resurrection."* The stone has been rolled away. There is no need for us to be defeated, we can go forward in the triumph of Jesus. We are fighting the enemy from the position of victory. This is not salvation that he is talking about here, albeit it is coming out of the bonds of death into newness of life. Yes, that is a spiritual awakening, but, this is a daily awareness of the risen life in our experience of God.

In ourselves, as Paul has detailed earlier, we can do nothing, we are nothing, we have nothing! So often we fail to cope with the conflicts of this life, we find it difficult to conquer the binding habits of sin, it is a struggle for us to live a life of purity and holiness. The way to do it is to draw on the resources we have in Christ i.e. His risen life. We are alive unto God!

Believe it or not, but the same power that God used to raise Jesus from the dead is available to each of us! Make sure your life is plugged in and switched on.

A passion worth sharing

Did you really notice what Paul prayed?

Sharing what? In His joys, in His triumphs, in His love and grace, in His many blessings ... oh yes! But, that was not what he prayed! He talks about *"sharing in His sufferings."*

He actually says more! He describes this as being *"fellowship."* I'm afraid our perception of fellowship is often from a slightly different perspective than this. Having said that, it really is a genuine privilege for us to suffer for Him, to bear the scars of battle, to know the pangs that rend the human heart, to feel the pain that can torment the body, to encounter the anguish that affliction can bring, to reel under the chilling wind of adversity - that, dear friend, is fellowship with Him in His sufferings. It means a cross.

The trials of life! What an honour to think that He counts us worthy to face them. You may not have seen it like that before, but that is fellowship with a capital F.

It will entail each of us taking up and bearing the cross in our lives. That will be a painful experience. It will take undiluted commitment. There is a price to pay, it will cost us dearly. We may be the butt of cynical jokes. Perhaps we may be subject to ridicule or even prone to ostracism. Possibly misunderstood. There is a reproach that has to be borne for the sake of our Lord Jesus.

A position worth seeking

The order that Paul has outlined in his prayer is worth noticing, he moves from a resurrection to a sacrifice to a death. It appears to be back to front, almost like putting the cart before the horse. The bottom line is that you can't have a resurrection without a death!

So he says, *"becoming like Him in His death."* This is a dying daily to self, sin and Satan. When we die to each of these influences in our lives then we become alive in Jesus. It is when "I" is dethroned and Christ is enthroned. It is when "I" am crucified and Christ is crowned. It is only when the corn of wheat falls into the ground and dies that it bears much fruit.

That's why He came. Calvary was the aim of the Incarnation. He was born to die. Then He died to live.

The same can be true in our lives if we are willing to endorse the sentiments expressed so movingly by the apostle: "Lord, I want to know you ..."

A praise worth anticipating

This is the only place in the New Testament where this form of the Greek word for *"resurrection"* is used. Literally it means "out-resurrection," the resurrection "out from the dead ones."

When the dead in Christ shall rise at the coming again of our Lord Jesus, the next event is the rewarding of the people of God at the judgment seat of Christ (cf. 2 Corinthians 5:10). Paul was speaking of that moment when he would stand before the Lord. He did not want to be empty-handed. He wanted to be able to offer Him fruit rather than nothing but leaves. It was Paul's hope and desire that at this particular time envisaged here he might receive a reward for his pursuit of the knowledge of Jesus Christ. In order to receive that reward in the next life, he would have to attain, or earn it, in this life. Part of that reward will be the ability to know Christ on the other side of death.

It all goes back to the moment in Paul's life when he realised the fallacy of being driven by confidence in the flesh as it was only taking him into a dead end street, a spiritual cul-de-sac. He found that his religion was just like an onion. When he peeled away layer upon layer of traditions, rules and regulations, he discovered to his horror that he had nothing. On the other hand, he found that Christianity was like a treasure chest. The outside may have looked quite unimpressive, but when he looked inside he was pleasantly surprised. He found a cross, an empty tomb, a promise of power, a hope of glory, riches beyond measure. And they were all embodied in one Person, the Lord Jesus Christ. He could happily identify with the observation of W. H. Griffith Thomas when he noted, "Christianity is nothing less and can be nothing more than relationship to Christ."

As Charles Swindoll says, "he wanted to spend the balance of his years on earth knowing Christ more intimately, drawing upon His resurrection power more increasingly, entering into His sufferings more personally, and being conformed to His image more completely. His dreams of making it all on his own were forever dashed on the solid rock of Jesus Christ."

I can't help but ask myself the question: "Am I staying too near where I got in?" Maybe you should do the same.

CHAPTER THIRTEEN

Going for gold ... and God

Going for gold! That is the aim and aspiration of the vast company of athletes who assemble every four years from all over the world to take part in the Olympic Games. For them, to stand on the winner's podium, hailed as a hero, with the strains of their home country's national anthem ringing in their ears, emotion etched on their tear stained faces, would make all the sacrifice and strenuous effort worthwhile.

You know, the Christian life is no different. Paul sees it as a race! It is not a 100 yard dash. It is a marathon cross-country. Of necessity, we are to abandon our own selfish ambitions so that we may wholeheartedly pursue the goal that is set before us. Nothing must hinder or hamper our steady progress. It is not a spectator sport but one of active participation by all. Down the straight, round the bend, over the hurdle, in the final analysis, consistency is what really matters.

There will be frustration as we strive to attain spiritual fitness. Many tears may be shed as we count the cost of getting rid of the excess baggage. The pain barrier must be broken if we are to keep on going. But, even though we may not all be winners by nature, with the spiritual instincts of the new man reigning within, we can conquer all and cross the finishing line in triumph.

Awaiting us is Christ, the One who has gone on before. No greater incentive can be given; no other motivation should be required. That's why we pull out all the stops, with every fibre of our being, stretching all the sinews, as we keep the end in view. What an exhilarating prospect.

Let's go for gold ... and ... go for God!

This was Paul's thinking. It was his game plan. And, he stuck rigidly to it. Like him, we want to be there at the end. Paul shows us how to do it in 3:12-16. He leaves us a few tips that are designed to enhance performance:

* be realistic - know where you are at

* be single minded - learn the art of concentration

* be forward looking - resist the temptation to look back

* be a plodder - don't be a dropout on the last lap

* be sensible - know the rules and stick to them

Winning moves. Yes! Absorb them and get yourself down to the track!

Number One: BE REALISTIC

"Not that I have already obtained all this, or have already been made perfect ... I do not consider myself yet to have taken hold of it" (3:12,13)

If the old adage is true, open confession is good for the soul, Paul will feel a lot better for having cleared his chest. He has come clean, and you can hardly believe what he says. It's a frank assessment of where he is at spiritually. Here is honesty clothed in humility.

He hasn't arrived. He hasn't reached his goal. He hasn't obtained his ambition. He hasn't achieved his target. What a relief to find that Paul has similar struggles to ourselves. Perfection eludes us. It can't be any other way. We live in an imperfect world. We are surrounded by imperfect people. We witness imperfections on a daily basis in every area of modern life. And it will continue to be like that until we reach heaven itself.

It is quite remarkable when we realise that the apostle Paul was at the zenith of his career and yet he realised that he had not reached the high-water mark of his calling. He had permeated major cities with the gospel, he had founded churches which continued to flourish, he had written major doctrinal letters which even today astound the scholars, but he was not satisfied with himself. The more he accomplished, the more he saw that needed to be accomplished. Not for him the easy way out of putting his feet up and resting on his laurels. You'll not find him reclining on a leather chair twiddling his thumbs in an attitude of smug temerity. Certainly not!

The picture here is of a man who is far from satisfied with his progress on the road that leads to Christ likeness. He freely admits that he is not perfect! There's room for improvement. There was still plenty of scope for advancement in many departments of his life. He has no illusions of grandeur about himself nor has he got rose tinted spectacles on when it comes to future growth in grace. He knows full well there is a long way to go.

He says: "Look, this is where I am ... that is where I am going ... and, in between, I have a lot to learn."

Number Two: BE SINGLE MINDED

"One thing I do" (3:13)

The temptation we all grapple with is to have too many irons in the fire. We were never meant to be a Jack-of-all-trades. God wants us to be master of one! Concentration is thereby essential. It is the name of the game. We should be immersed in one thing and invest our energy towards its final accomplishment. We should be keen to see it through to the end and not let anyone or anything distract us. Remember Nehemiah on the building site in Jerusalem. This was the spirit he portrayed: *"I am doing a great work so that I cannot come down"* (Nehemiah 6:3). It's all about being focussed and having the ability to home in on the target with precision and dedication.

At the end of the day, it is a matter of personal values, of getting our priorities right, of sorting out the agenda of our lives. We need to always remember that the most important thing is to ensure that the most important thing remains the most important thing.

Number Three: BE FORWARD LOOKING

"forgetting what is behind" (3:13)

The phrase that Paul employs here is one that is borrowed from the world of athletics. It was used of a runner who outran another in the same race. Once he got into the lead, he would never turn and look back; he would forget about the other runner. The one in the lead focuses on the tape before him rather than the other runners behind him.

What a challenge this is to all of us, you can't live your life looking over your shoulder. The past is behind us and it cannot be changed. We can't rewrite the history of our lives. It happened yesterday, we should be content to leave it there. We can all learn from the past but how foolish it is to live in the past.

The apostle is encouraging us to forget about our past failures. So often when we think about them we plunge into the depths of despair and we become defeatist in our outlook. The past can give us a mental block. It can colour our perception of the present and can taint our better sense of judgment. It can shackle us and lead us into bondage. Instead of the past being an instrument to teach us beneficial lessons it can quickly become an influence that terrorises us. If we are going to be successful in our quest for gold we will need to stay in the right lane on the right track, a walk into the past will only succeed in derailing and demoralising us. Such memories will only haunt us, not help us.

It is equally true to say, we should also forget about our past successes. If we don't it would be dangerously easy for us to become complacent and relax our spiritual training programme. Grateful, yes. Proud, no. We can't live on the blessing of yesterday's triumphs. Today is another day. There are new challenges and fresh opportunities, if we are genuinely going for gold we will be looking ahead.

I read recently a comment which made me sit up and take notice. It said, "A leader of the persecuted church once said that 95 percent of the believers who face the test of persecution, pass it, while 95 percent of the believers who face the test of prosperity, fail it."

The parting shot is this: if we keep remembering our successes, we will soon have nothing to remember.

Number Four: BE A PLODDER

"I press on to take hold of that for which Christ Jesus took hold of me ... straining towards what is ahead, I press on towards the goal to win

the prize for which God has called me heavenwards in Christ Jesus" (3:12-14)

It is highly likely when Paul was penning these words that he had a picture in his mind's eye of the chariot races that were so popular in the Olympic Games. Charles Swindoll reminds us, "he could have been thinking of the chariot racer standing in that small, two wheeled cart with long, leather reins in his hands, leaning forward to keep his balance."

This was not a sport for the fainthearted. It was for those who were willing to risk life and limb in order to claim the garland at the end of the race. Such should be our experience in life, we are to keep our eyes directly ahead of us in anticipation of the day when we will cross the finishing line. From here to there, the best line to follow is that of our putting everything into it. Anything less will result in our coming unstuck. That's too high a price to pay.

Another fascinating simile is adopted by Paul in his use of the terms, *"to take hold of ... took hold of me."* It is the picture of the rugby player who runs someone down from behind and tackles him so that he might get his hands on the ball. Paul wanted to experience everything that God had for his life, and he was eager to grab hold of all that God put in front of him.

We can also detect in the phrase, *"pressing on towards the goal,"* an allusion to an athlete on the track. The verb reminds us of someone who runs without swerving off course, straining every nerve and muscle as he keeps on running with all his might toward the goal.

Whichever comparison you may prefer to personalise, all that matters is that we keep on going to the very end of the race. Sadly, too many fall out on the last lap. They drop out and fail to finish. It all becomes too much for them. They're the losers.

When weariness invades our body, when the pain barrier needs to be crossed, when the odds are stacked even higher than the hurdles, when we're hurt in the fray at the many bends on the track, when we're elbowed and we lose our wind for a time, when we're spiked and spill blood in the process, when we trip and fall in the dust, we must keep going.

Why? The answer is obvious. It's all about securing the prize at the end of the race. It's the reward at the end of it that makes it all worthwhile. The victor's wreath. A word of commendation. A crown which will never fade. This is the sole reason for our calling, heavenly and high as it is. You see, in Paul's thinking, the goal and the prize were one and the same, He is the Prize.

Number Five: BE SENSIBLE

"All of us who are mature should take such a view of things. And if on some point you think differently, that too God will make clear to you. Only let us live up to what we have already attained" (3:15,16)

What Paul is instructing us about here is really a matter of common sense. But sometimes sense is not very common. He says we should abide by the rules and not seek to find a way around them. If we want to hold our heads up high as we cross the finishing line then obedience to the rules is absolutely essential. We should never seek to infringe the guidelines set out before us. Who wants to be disqualified? Who wants to be shown the red card?

Sadly, the track is littered with people who began the race with enormous potential but they failed at the end because they broke the rules. I recall the likes of Lot, Samson, Saul, Ananias, Sapphira, and Demas, to name but a few. Oh yes, they were competing, but they were in a different race! They were left with red faces and with their heads buried in their hands.

This is the policy that Paul adhered to and which he feels strongly is the line that mature believers should similarly adopt. There will be those who have other ideas. Paul is happy to agree to differ with them because he knows that God will have the last word.

The final sentence in verse 16 is a timely challenge to all those in the church at Philippi and since then not to throw out the baby with the bath water. They have come so far. They have done so well. They have made up a lot of ground. They have everything to live for. Says Paul, "don't be foolish and throw it all away in a moment of reckless abandon." They would be crazy if they allowed themselves to become sidetracked at such a critical moment. The finishing line would disappear over the horizon and they would be the ultimate losers. They are to persevere with gritted teeth and honest endeavour. Heads down. Eyes front. Moving forward. One step at a time.

In going for gold they are going for God ..!

CHAPTER FOURTEEN

Paul - the great visionary

"You can tell the character of a man by what it takes to stop him."

Of course that statement needs some qualifications, for we need to make sure that a person's goals are worthy before we talk about the toughness of character that keeps him going, no matter what. When the going gets tough, the tough get going! The fact is that some good men could have been great men if they had not stopped so soon.

Though we often see cowardice in the lives of others, it is not so easily detected in ourselves. It's the "speck of sawdust in your brother's eye and the plank in your own eye" syndrome.

Apparently in one of his long speeches to the Supreme Soviet, Khrushchev was severely critical of Joseph Stalin to such an extent that someone from the floor of the hall sent up a note for the Premier to read. It's caustic message came in the form of a question: "What were you doing when Stalin committed all those atrocities?"

"Who sent up this note?" Khrushkev shouted.

Not a person stirred. There was an eerie silence.

"I'll give him one minute to stand up!"

Still no-one moved as the seconds ticked away. Time was running out.

"Alright, I'll tell you what I was doing," Khrushkev began. "I was doing what the writer of this note was doing - *nothing!* I was afraid to be counted!"

Paul was a man who was willing to be counted. He could not be stopped. He had a dozen reasons why he could have chosen an early retirement. He could have spent his remaining years writing his memoirs. But, he didn't. Why? Because, he had a goal in view. He had a sense of destiny. He was on a mission and the job was still not done. He never lost his vision, it never became blurred.

Warren Wiersbe has described Paul in chapter 3 as being an accountant with a new set of values (vs. 1-11); an athlete with vigour and vitality (vs. 12-16); and, an alien with a fresh vision (vs. 17-21).

So, what does this man of vision have to say to us as we rapidly approach the end of the twentieth century?

HE LEAVES AN EXAMPLE

"Join with others in following my example, brothers, and take note of those who live according to the pattern we gave you" (3:17)

Have you read it right? Did you really see what Paul was saying? He's a brave man. A courageous man. He's not being foolhardy. He's certainly not conceited. Nor is he going on an ego trip to increase the measurement of his head. He simply says: "Do as I do" and "Do as I say."

He is encouraging them to mimic his example. If they do their lives will be better for it. They need to keep on walking with God, keep on growing in Christ, keep on climbing in their pursuit of God. The encouraging fact is that they will not be alone, there are others on the same pilgrimage. And, his example is not the only one worth imitating, there are others whose lives can be admired and appreciated.

His was a lifestyle worth duplicating, his was an example worth copying. It would be good for them to see him as a role model. They would retain their own sense of identity, they would still be themselves and not a shadow of someone else. He was not expecting them to become replicas in Philippi of himself. They would hold on to their individual personality but each of them would be marching to the drumbeat of Jesus. And, they would find Paul in step to the same tune.

Men followers! Maybe. In following Paul they were walking in the footsteps of Jesus. As they followed the missionaries so they followed the Master. The reason why Paul was able to give such an exhortation was because of his closeness to Christ, his communion with Christ, and his consecration to Christ.

His conduct was exemplary. Oh, that we were able to say the same as Paul said to our peers. It is impossible to assess the power of a godly example.

HE LISTS OUR ENEMIES

"For, as I have often told you before and now say again even with tears, many live as enemies of the cross of Christ" (3:18)

We caught a glimpse of Paul in the previous verse as a brave man, now we see him as a broken man with tears in his eyes. He's weeping. He is overcome with emotion as his heart rends at the prospect of some of the members of the church at Philippi becoming ensnared with a first century personality cult. He breaks down as he contemplates the lostness of these pseudo saints. They are synthetic saints and spiritual masqueraders. They look genuine but they lack reality. They pose as friends but they practice as foes, they are enemies.

There were two groups of tricksters who had infiltrated the ranks of the people of God. These were the Judaisers and the Antinomians. Their policy is fairly straightforward and can be summarised in a few words. The former group are the Party of the Law where nothing goes! The latter are renowned as the Party of Liberty where anything and everything goes!

He says three things about them:

their doom

"their destiny is destruction" (3:19)

What an awful end awaits those who know not Jesus as Lord and Saviour. This is their future. Eternal hopelessness. Hell. Wasted lives. Their goal is perdition where they will be banished from the presence of God forever. They are mere professors with a religion that is empty.

their deity

"their god is their stomach, and their glory is in their shame" (3:19)

They are wrapped up in themselves and have immersed their lives in fleshly affairs. They are driven by sensual appetites and have no hangups about their lack of moral purity. They are totally absorbed in the rigid regime of dietary laws as they pampered themselves and pandered to their every whim and fantasy. They are carnal and corrupt. Their life revolved around matters of time and doing their own thing. They had a perverted sense of values as sensuality was the fuel that lit their fires.

their disposition

"their mind is on earthly things" (3:19)

Here's the tell-tale factor. Everyone has a grid or mindset through which he makes major decisions. That grid determines his life. Paul's grid was heaven and theirs was the earth. They are earthed to this present world. They are earth dwellers, earth bound, and earth oriented. They were materialistic and could see no further than the here and now. Their view was all soil and no sky.

HE LOOKS WITH EXPECTANCY

"But our citizenship is in heaven. And we eagerly await a Saviour from there, the Lord Jesus Christ, who, by the power that enables Him to bring everything under His control, will transform our lowly bodies so that they will be like His glorious body" (3:20,21)

What a contrast between them and us is seen in the use of the word *"but."* We live down here on planet earth but we really belong to another world. We pitch the tent of our lives down here but we're not getting our roots down. We're just passing through as this world is not our home, we're only here as temporary tenants as our main residence is in heaven. We're not settlers. We are pilgrims in transit.

Yes, we're here, and at the same time, we're there! We are in two places at once! The locals would be familiar with such an analogy as Philippi was a Roman colony. The inhabitants of Philippi were looked upon as Roman citizens even though Rome was a fair distance from them. The same can be said for the people of God, we're here but we belong elsewhere.

This is the pioneer spirit that captivated the imagination and harnessed the energy of so many who have gone before us. I think of father Abraham who looked for a city and was content to live in a tent. When he started out on his voyage of discovery he left no forwarding address. Moses springs to mind as one who looked for the rewards of heaven so he was happy to forsake the treasures of Egypt. He saw the invisible, chose the imperishable and did the impossible. The supreme example is our Lord Jesus who because of the joy that was before Him was willing to endure the Cross.

That is the ethos of Christianity. We should be ready to move at a moment's notice. For Christ is returning, soon, suddenly, surely. There should be an eagerness in our outlook with our hearts beating faster every passing day. His advent is imminent. He could break through the clouds at any moment and we will want to be ready to meet Him.

The Christ who comes is ...

the Christ who calls

He is coming from *"there"* to here for each of us who know Him personally. He is returning so that He might take us home to heaven to spend eternity in His presence. This is phase one of the advent of Christ, it is when He comes to the air for His people.

the Christ who controls

Phase two of His advent programme is when He returns to earth with His people. He is coming to rule and reign. He will be seen to exercise sovereign control over the world, His enemies will become His footstool, the earth will become His kingdom, He will crush the opposition, and He will subdue all the tyranny of evil.

the Christ who changes

The unchanging Christ in that day will become the all-changing Christ in that He will *"transform our lowly bodies so that they will be like His glorious body."* In a moment, faster than the batting of an eyelid, we will be changed to become like Jesus. Writing in a similar vein to the church at Corinth, the apostle said that our bodies will be buried in decay and raised without decay; they will be sown in humiliation and raised in splendour; they will be sown in weakness and raised in strength; they will be sown a physical body and raised a spiritual body (cf. 1 Corinthians 15).

A real body. A redeemed body. A recognisable body. For we shall know each other in heaven and we shall know as we are known. Then, and not before, the good work begun at our conversion will be complete (cf. Philippians 1:6). We are destined for the throne.

What a vision Paul has of the future for the believer. What a vista he gives us of the unfolding purpose of God. It's probably right and proper that we should pause for a moment and pray with John on the isle of Patmos: *"Even so, come, Lord Jesus!"* That's why he is living his life in the future tense.

And, that realisation means Paul is aware of his responsibilities in his present environment. We are here because God has placed us here. And until He comes and takes us out of the world we have an obligation resting on our shoulders to reach those whom he calls *"enemies of the cross of Christ."*

A story about Oliver Cromwell illustrates what God wants us to do in the time that is remaining to us prior to His advent. At the time, England was running out of silver for making coins. So Cromwell sent his men to the cathedrals to see if they could find any silver there. They reported, "The only silver we could find is in the statues of the saints standing in the corners" - to which the crusty statesman replied, "Good! We'll melt down the saints and put them into circulation!"

That's where we all belong, in circulation! We don't belong in the corner of some church building, gathering dust. We belong out among people. We have a message worth sharing. We have a mandate from heaven. We have a mission not yet finished. We are the men whom God is looking to so that the great task of reaching a world without Jesus might progress with speed.

There are some people who look at the way things are and ask, Why?

There are other people who look at the way things could be and ask, Why not? In the light of Paul's challenge, where do you see yourself fitting in?

Surely, we need to be a *"sunrise"* people - dreaming of the future; not a *"sunset"* people - dreaming of the past!

CHAPTER FIFTEEN

People are problems

A trip to Amsterdam is not complete without a visit to the famous Rijksmuseum. For a few guilders you can have the benefit of a tour guide with all his expertise. During the course of his running commentary he will inform you of an amazing statistic that about 10 percent of Rembrandt's paintings were paintings of himself. But far from being an exercise in self-aggrandisement, Rembrandt was a humble person who painted himself just as he was, with no embellishments. Artists have often wondered why he did not take advantage of his gifted hand and paint himself with just a touch of flattery, since his physical form was far from handsome. But Rembrandt remarked, "Unless I can paint myself just as I am, I cannot paint others as they are."

In the previous three chapters of his epistle we have seen the apostle in his true colours. Now, in his final chapter, he draws a picture for us of life in the first century in the church at Philippi. Stroke after stroke on the canvas of Scripture he paints it as it is.

There were people there. And, where you have people, you have problems!

I love the rather personal story recounted by Warren Wiersbe when he writes:

> My daughter jumped off the school bus as it stopped in front of our house and slammed her way through the front door. She marched defiantly up the stairs into her room and again

slammed the door. All the time she was muttering under her breath, "People - people - *people* - PEOPLE!"

I went to her door and knocked softly. "May I come in?"

She replied, "No!"

I tried again, but she said it even more belligerently: "NO!"

I asked, "Why can't I come in?"

Her answer: "Because you're a people!"

It's the kind of event that happens every day all across the country. We know exactly how he felt, and, we know exactly how she felt. Sometimes, people can have that effect upon us. It's most unpleasant.

In a *Peanuts* cartoon, Lucy says to Snoopy: "There are times when you really bug me, but I must admit there are also times when I feel like giving you a big hug."

Snoopy replies: "That's the way I am ... huggable and buggable!"

And so it is with our relationships within the local church family. There were obvious tensions within the church and people were beginning to take sides. Fragmentation seemed inevitable. It's hard to comprehend, but back in the first century when life was relatively simple and everyone's pace was so much slower, there were still childish squabbles. Sadly some people have nothing better to do with their time than waste it nitpicking and majoring on minors. To an outsider looking in it would all appear so embarrassingly petty. It was the "sledgehammer to crack a nut" syndrome that seemed to be prevalent. It was both needless and senseless.

So Paul, in the next few verses, is attempting to put out the fires that are blazing. He is seeking to defuse the timebomb of disharmony. That is the root problem from which there have sprung three areas of pastoral concern:

THEY WERE DEFEATIST

"Therefore, my brothers, you whom I love and long for, my joy and

crown, that is how you should stand firm in the Lord, dear friends" (4:1)

Paul has a wonderful way of describing people. He can really make you feel good. He boosts their morale as he affirms them for who they are, he speaks of them in a fourfold manner.

He calls them *"brothers"* and this would indicate they were all members of the same family. He looked upon them as his spiritual brothers and sisters. A most interesting phrase is used when he refers to them as *"my joy"* - this is a reminder to them of the tremendous joy they have brought into his life. They are like the icing on the cake of his Christian experience. *"My crown"* is a reference to what they will be in a day to come. He has led them to the Lord and at the judgment seat of Christ he will receive a soul-winner's crown. They will be the sparkling jewels in that crown. What a fitting reward for a man who was instrumental in their conversion. He talks about them being his *"dear friends"* and this is suggestive of the love that binds their hearts together. He is happy and relaxed when sharing with them because he really enjoys their fellowship, they mean so much to him.

Paul bares his heart as he says, *"I love you and I long for you"* - he values them as people for who they are. He accepts them. He is enamoured with them and so the terms of endearment flow easily and naturally.

Having reassured them of his affection he then proceeds to challenge them to *"stand firm in the Lord."* You see, some of them were beginning to ping under the pressure they were encountering. They were on the verge of giving up and giving in. It would have been easy for them to yield ground to the enemy. Retreat seemed a viable alternative as they thought to themselves: if you can't stand the heat, get out of the kitchen! Looking at the situation from an objective perspective, these were all soft options.

The first signs of instability were beginning to appear, the dreaded cracks were making an unwelcome entry into the life of the fellowship. There was an air of gloom and despondency as one after another adopted a defeatist mentality. Says Paul, *"stand firm."*

Their power base is *"in the Lord."* This particular expression is found no fewer than eight times in Paul's letter, He is the secret of their strength and security. He is their source of power. All the way through Paul's note to the church the focus has been not on our circumstances or on others or on ourselves, but on the Lord. Their eyes should be looking only to Him. He will enable them to go on. If they pick up the broken pieces in their relationships He will put them back together again, they're family. They're in it together!

This concept of standing firm is one of the apostle's hobby horses. He often writes along these lines. For example:

"stand firm in the faith" (1 Corinthians 16:13)

"stand firm in your freedom" (Galatians 5:1)

"stand firm on your foundation" (2 Thessalonians 2:15)

In this verse he reminds them to *"stand firm in the family"* - together they can face the foe. They were on the winning team. Therefore, it was imperative that they be positive in their outlook. Victory is certain!

THEY WERE DIVIDED

Here is public enemy number one and Paul puts his finger on it straightaway. He calls a spade, "a spade" not a "sharp edged gardening implement" as he bravely tackles the thorny problem in the life of the fellowship. He says:

"I plead with Euodia and I plead with Syntyche to agree with each other in the Lord" (4:2)

How tragic! Two ladies had fallen out. They were at loggerheads. Something had happened between them to sour their relationship. We don't know what the specific problem was but it was enough to put up a barrier between them. They aren't on speaking terms any longer. Previously they had been the best of friends, now they can't stand the sight of each other. Oh yes, they were adults in age and height, but they were awfully childish in their attitudes.

To add fuel to the fire, these women were not just happy-clappy pew warmers. No! They had been actively involved in the work of God. They had shared fellowship with Paul and had been a tremendous asset to him. Many were the times they had worked side by side with each other and with him so as to ensure the furtherance of the gospel. He says that they have *"contended at my side in the cause of the gospel"* (4:3).

Then the enemy fired a poisoned dart that permeated their relationship. They clashed. Tempers flared. They boiled over. Words were said. Sparks were flying. Result: two lives poles apart. And the ripples are such that it reaches beyond the small radius of their relationship. It spills over and adversely affects the whole church family to a greater or lesser degree.

They have it in for each other. None will give ground. They stand on their own rights. They stick to their guns. None is prepared to say, "Look, I'm sorry ..." They dig their stiletto heels in and walk about with a large chip on their shoulders. It's a grudge match.

Here was a church which in the goodness of God had been started by women was now being torn apart because of two headstrong women. They obviously were not living up to their names. Euodia means "sweet fragrance" and Syntyche means "affable." So disruptive was the controversy raging between the two of them that someone has suggested that if the Philippians were Paul's crown, Euodia and Syntyche had become two thorns in that crown! I suppose we could rename them ... Euodia would become *Odious* and Syntyche would become *Soon Touchy!*

Sad, isn't it? Mature ladies acting like spoilt children!

He passionately pleads with them. He urges them. He implores them to patch up their differences and be friends again. He doesn't take sides and blame one or the other. He has been around long enough to know that it takes two to tango. There are always faults on both sides. The road leading to a breakdown in harmony is never a one way street. Both of them are to blame for what has happened. Both are, therefore, responsible to see that it gets sorted out.

They need to get off their high horses and step down to reality. They need to back down and swallow their pride. They need to sit down and talk again. They may need to eat humble pie if they are to banish their feelings of resentment. They need to meet on a common piece of ground which Paul says is *"in the Lord."* Life's far too short to hold spite against each other in the family of God. They may not see eye to eye but they can still disagree without being disagreeable. They can forgive each other and start again. A dislocated member of the body is of little use, he wants them to be back in fellowship and restored to their former usefulness. He wants to see them back again in their proper place, not out of joint! Let's face it, they're the ones that are losing out. As Charles Swindoll says, "The peace and contentment and joy that could be theirs was draining away, like water down the drain of an unplugged bathtub."

Paul was realistic enough to know that if they couldn't get together and sort the problem out between themselves then it may take a Christian equivalent of ACAS. A third person may be needed to act as a kind of arbitrator. This is the one Paul refers to as a *"loyal yokefellow"* (4:3). He would be a mediator or a middleman. He would have the best interests of the fellowship at heart so he would be an ideal go-between. His aim would be reconciliation.

Many words have been written over the years as commentators have tried to track this individual down. They have tried to identify him and the various conclusions reached are on a sliding scale that goes from the sublime to the ridiculous. One of the most reasonable and believable is the one that William Hendricksen subscribes to. He thinks Paul was using a play on words:

> In all probability ... the apostle is making use of a play on a name, for Syzygus means Yokefellow, a person who pulls well in a harness for two, and Paul is saying that Syzygus was true to his name ... It is safe to infer that Syzygus, about whom we have no further information, was one of Paul's comrades or associates in the work of the gospel. When this letter was written he was a prominent member of the church at Philippi, a man of influence who was highly esteemed by his people.

> Like the apostle himself, he must have been a man of extraordinary tact. Otherwise Paul would not have requested him to lend a hand in restoring harmony between the two women.

He may be right. He may be wrong. It doesn't really matter. But, it's an interesting line of thought. What is clear is that this man would have had a real job on his hands that would take considerable tenderness and tact combined with a prayerful and gracious attitude.

We have no way of knowing the outcome of this meeting of minds. The sequel has not been written. Time will tell. Eternity will reveal all. Hopefully, it will have been blessed with a measure of success.

Let me illustrate:

The story is told of two porcupines who were huddled close together on a bitterly cold night up in northern Canada. The closer they got to stay warm, the more their quills pricked each other, making it virtually impossible for them to remain side by side. Silently, they moved apart. Before long, they were shivering in the wintry gale, so they came back together. Soon both were poking and jabbing each other ... so they separated again. Same story. Same result. Their action was repeated all night long - back and forth, back and forth.

Our two friends, Euodia and Syntyche were like the Canadian porcupines; they needed each other, but they kept needling each other.

Point made!

THEY WERE DEPRESSED

Problem no. 1 meant some of them were in danger of losing ground. Problem no. 2 reminds us that a couple of them were losing face. Now, when we tackle problem no. 3, we discover that there were those who were losing heart.

They were discouraged and disheartened. They had opened the window of their lives and joy had flown. Their smile has gone. Their enthusiasm has dissipated. Their energy is waning. Their sense of excitement has all but evaporated. They're on a downer. It's the whatever-day-of-the-week-it-is blues! They feel drained and exhausted. They're running on empty. They are harassed and are showing classic symptoms of the "washed out and hanging on the line to dry" syndrome.

There were many problems from without that we have looked at in our earlier studies; their situation was exacerbated, however, because of the festering problem of disunity within. As is so often the case, they are the casualties caught up in the crossfire between the warring factions.

To these weary pilgrims Paul writes a prescription that will lift their hearts and set them back reinvigorated on the road to recovery. He says: *"rejoice in the Lord always. I will say it again: Rejoice!"* (4:4).

Rejoice! He doesn't only say it once. He says it a second time: rejoice! It is not an optional extra. It is not an elective in God's school. It is a command to be obeyed. Not just some of the time when we are in the mood to do it and we have that "feel good" factor in our lives. But, all of the time!

Paul is reminding them that they should not let things get them down or allow people to rob them of their joy. Their joy is focussed and centred in Jesus. Happiness depends on happenings, but even when everything is falling apart they can still experience joy. The problem is that some Christian's have a joy that is so deep, it never rises to the surface!

Humanly speaking, that is not easy to do. It goes against the grain. But our joy is in the Lord. It is not in our changing circumstances, nor is it in our fluctuating fortunes as life can sometimes be like the proverbial yo-yo. It's in the Lord! He remains constant. He is unchanging. We can be radiant even though we may feel rotten inside - our joy *is* Jesus.

When we cultivate a joyfulness in the Lord we will bounce back to where we once were with God. It's almost like the Comeback Kid philosophy, no matter how deflated we may feel there's always a way back when we start praising Him for who He is. When the once silent chord begins to vibrate again in our lives it will prove to be a marvellous antidote to all our cares and concerns.

This joy will be conspicuous, continuous and contagious.

It will be heard in our song. It will be seen in the twinkle in our eye. It will be recognised by the warm glow of our personality. It will add an extra yard to our every footstep.

Yes, people are problems! We need to stand together (vs. 1), think together (vs. 2), work together (vs. 3), and praise Him together (vs. 4).

And so, says Paul, whatever the problem may be, whoever the people may be, we should be living a life of continual rejoicing!

How about starting ... now!

CHAPTER SIXTEEN

Big hearted Christians

Are you into chess?

I came across a story recently that captured my imagination. In the early part of the last century an artist painted a picture of a chess game. The players were a young man and Satan. The young man manipulated the white pieces, Satan the black ones. If the young man were to win, he would be forever free from the power of evil; if Satan were to win, the young man would be his servant forever.

The artist, who was a great chess player, had the pieces lines up in such a way that the devil had just moved his queen and announced checkmate in four moves. The young man was seen hovering over his rook, his face pale with fear.

For years the picture hung in an art gallery with chess players from all over the world coming to ponder the configuration of the pieces, convinced that the devil had won. Yet one day a famous chess player named Paul Morphy was brought into the gallery to view the picture. He stood there, gesturing with his hands, as in his imagination he eliminated one move after another. To the amazement of all, the old man figured out a combination of moves that would defeat the devil.

"Young man, make that move!" he shouted.

Just when you and I think the devil has outplayed us, God reminds us that there is a move we can make. The enemy may shout "Checkmate!" But God can show us a move we can make that has not crossed the enemy's mind.

And, here it is in verses 5 to 9. It's a positive course of action that Paul is advocating we should take. He begins by breaking new ground. He says: *"let your gentleness be evident to all"* (4:5). That is a most unusual word. I understand this is the only time it is used in the New Testament, in the A.V. it is translated "moderation."

It means "forbearance" or "sweet reasonableness." A modern idiom would be "easygoing."

The kind of person Paul sees here is someone who is easy to get along with, someone in whose company you can relax and feel at home, someone who will bring out the best in you, someone who is generous in spirit, someone who is kind and considerate, the genial sort of individual. He's talking about the fella or girl who is good-natured and good-humoured.

Here is a cameo of a big hearted Christian.

* They have a heart for people ...

* They have a heart for the lost ...

* And, they have a heart for God.

Big hearted: that's the secret to a life in touch and in tune with God.

* It's a heart that reaches up to heaven ...

* It's a heart that reaches down to those in need ...

* It's a heart that reaches out to those around us.

What do big hearted Christian's have about them that causes you to sit up and take notice? What is their common denominator?

THEY ENJOY THE PRESENCE OF GOD

"the Lord is near" (4:5)

They revel in the nearness of Jesus. He is at hand. He is close by. By faith, they can reach out and touch Him. The old Quakers put it well when they said: "the Lord is at your elbow." Yes, He's as near as that!

There are many lonely people in today's world, many feel hemmed in, cut off and isolated from their friends and family. They feel boxed in. They spend long tedious hours with their own company. To all such, the Lord is near. In the best of times, the Lord is with us; and, in the worst of times, the Lord is still with us. In every circumstance of life, in every changing season of life, He is a friend at all times. He isn't only present when the sun is shining, He's there when the tempest is raging and it's blowing a gale. The weather makes no difference to Him. He's there!

He is One who stands up for us ...

He is One who stands with us ...

And, He is One who stands by us ... rejoice!

THEY ENGAGE THE POWER OF GOD

"do not be anxious about anything, but in everything, by prayer and petition, with thanksgiving, present your requests to God" (4:6)

"Why pray when you can worry" seems to be the norm for many of us. But, the person Paul is thinking about here is someone who taps the potential of heaven. They explore the possibilities open to them as they storm the gates of glory. They prove that God hears and answers prayer. The big hearted Christian takes his burden to the Lord and leaves it there.

How often do we come before the Lord with our nagging worries and after a few minutes of prayer we get up from our knees and pick up our bag of cares and walk away with them again? Says Paul, why worry when you can pray!

We get our English word *worry* from the German word *wurgen* which means "to strangle, to choke." Our Lord used the same word picture on one occasion when He related the story of the sower, the seed and the soils (cf. Mark 4:14-19). That's what worry does. It cuts off our life-line and blocks the airways in our life. We feel as if someone has tied a ligature around our neck. The effect is devastating. The consequences are serious.

Spiritually, worry assaults our faith, and we end up in a fog of doubt that blurs the face of God. Physically, it steals our health, many of the medical problems that ravage our bodies are stress induced. Emotionally, it destroys our peace; the serenity necessary for a normal life evaporates.

Someone has said that "worry is when we pay the interest on trouble before the bill comes due."

What are the alternatives to worry?

Paul says quite simply that we should worry about nothing and pray about everything. We should make prayer a priority rather than see it as a last resort. We are to stop fumbling with our worry beads and begin talking our burdens over with the Lord. He wants to do the worrying for us! And, when we offload them on to His shoulders, anxiety will drain from our hearts like water from a sieve.

Billy Graham's wife often tells the story of the weary Christian who lay awake at night trying to hold the world together by his worrying. One night he heard the Lord gently say to him, "Now you go to sleep, Jim; I'll sit up."

"O what peace we often forfeit, O what needless pain we bear,
All because we do not carry, Everything to God in prayer."

"Everything" means everything! The big things in life as well as the small insignificant issues. No matter what it is God wants to hear about it. He really is interested. If it affects you, it greatly concerns Him. Why should we deprive Him of the privilege of sharing with us in our tension packed moments?

The way to ward off worry is to switch our needs from our worry list to our prayer list. Paul tells us how to do it:

"by prayer" - this is when we bring our requests to the throne of grace. It carries with it the idea of adoration, devotion and worship. It is when we see the greatness and grandeur of God. It is when we come face to face with His majesty and we sense that He is bigger than all our problems.

"and petition" - this is supplication which is an earnest seeking after God. It is sincere. It is spiritual conflict and highlights the intensity of our praying. An example of such an encounter is where Christ is praying in the garden of Gethsemane. It is urgent, specific and particular prayer. It is not going around the world for a short-cut, it is straight to the point.

"thanksgiving" - is to be mingled with our asking. This is when we have a profound sense of appreciation for who He is and for all that He has done for us. Our prayer is to be accompanied with a spirit of gratitude. Praise springs from an awareness of the goodness and many mercies of God.

Be careful for nothing ...

Be prayerful for everything ...

Be thankful for anything ...

THEY EXPERIENCE THE PEACE OF GOD

Paul is speaking here about something which all of us want but few of us have, it is peace. Peace with God. Peace with ourselves. Peace with our partner. Peace with our friends and colleagues. Peace with our past, our present and our future.

Peace. The undisturbableness of God reigning in our lives. It is far more wonderful than the human mind can understand. It is incomprehensible. It surpasses our wildest dreams. A Scotsman would say it is better felt than telt!

When we stop worrying and start praying then we experience His peace in our hearts and minds. Away with all our fears! Banish all our cares! We wave them farewell. And we receive the peace of God. What welcome relief!

"and the peace of God, which transcends all understanding, will guard your hearts and your minds in Christ Jesus" (4:7)

The apostle sees it as a garrison for the heart and a guard for the mind. It is something to be experienced today in the hour of trial or triumph, in moments of pain or pleasure, in seasons of sorrow or joy.

This peace is a sentinel at the door of the heart and mind. It is there all day and all night. Twenty four hours a day. Week in. Week out. Month after month. Year after year. When Satan would try to attack us and invade our lives then the sentry is on duty. Colonel Peace is standing guard. He keeps watch and deters any intruder from a forced entry. He is a kind of spiritual surveillance system to monitor our hearts. Thank God, He never fails!

It is a quiet confidence in Him, a relaxing in His love and a resting in His caring arms; it is that inner composure which only comes when we are fully trusting in Him. The storm may be hurricane force on the outside but we have a deep calm on the inside. It is designed for the heart as it will protect us from wrong feelings. And, it is tailor-made for the mind to protect us from wrong thinking. It is in the words of Isaiah, *"perfect peace."*

THEY ENCOURAGE THE PURSUIT OF GOD

It's all in the mind. Paul reminds us of the need to think with a clear mind and a clean mind. You may be familiar with the saying: "You are not what you think you are; but what you think - you are." That puts the ball back into our court, we may not be able to select our circumstances but we can choose our attitude. Here we have a menu for the mind. If we follow the apostle's guidelines then we will continue to win the war over worry. Thinking right and right thinking fit hand in glove. He says, *"finally, brothers ... think about such things"* (4:8).

What things? There are six items on his list:

"whatever is true"

We are to think about that which is genuine and sincere. We are to focus our minds on facts in preference to that which is deceptive or illusory. This is not fantasy or imagination run riot, we shouldn't live in a dream world of make-believe but in a real world of holding on to that which is reliable.

"whatever is noble"

This is no pat-on-the-head salesman's spiel. It is that which is honourable and above board. It is something which is worthy of reverence because it has the dignity of holiness stamped upon it. Honesty is not the best policy for the Christian, in this context, it is the only policy.

"whatever is right"

It is that which is upright, just and fair. It will have no time to think about rumours or malicious scandal or idle gossip. If it's wrong it can't be right! It is a conversation or train of thought which God would approve of.

"whatever is pure"

In a murky world we should seek to be above and beyond reproach in our thought life. A wholesome and healthy outlook is envisaged in this phrase. In an age when anything passes as acceptable we need to guard our minds from harbouring such filth and dirt. We should not allow our minds to dwell on that which is smutty, shabby or soiled lest we become defiled.

"whatever is lovely"

This would remind us of those things which are amiable, pleasing and agreeable. It is that which is commendable and beautiful. It is attractive and catches the eye and in so doing brings honour and glory to the name of Jesus. It is pleasing.

"whatever is admirable"

The encouragement here is to fix our minds on those things which are of good report. They are virtuous. It is the epitome of graciousness and stands in stark contrast to the that's-just-me-and-people-can-take-it-or-leave-it attitude so often prevalent today.

What a list! But, he's not finished yet. He picks up all six suggestions and places them in one basket and says, *"if anything is excellent or praiseworthy"* think about it! Go for quality every time.

Well, it's all about our thought lives. How we think is important. About ourselves, about others, about God.

When we are thinking right then we will be in pursuit of God.

THEY ARE EXAMPLES TO THE PEOPLE OF GOD

"Whatever you have learned or received or heard from me, or seen in me - put it into practice" (4:9)

Paul says, you have seen me, heard me, received from me, learned from me, now, go out and live for God. It is putting into practice what we have been taught. It is all about learning and living the Christian life. It is doing what God asks us to do and being what God wants us to be. It is not all theory. It works in the real world.

We don't want to be like the preacher of whom it was said, "He preached so well in the pulpit that it was a tragedy for him ever to go out of it, but he lived so poorly that it was unfortunate that he ever entered it."

Paul's parting shot reminds us of the priceless bonus given to those who are not held captive by the chains of tension or preoccupied with worry. This is the promise God makes to all those who have moved on from the "today is the tomorrow you worried about yesterday" mindset to living "one day at a time."

"and the God of peace will be with you" (4:9)

Yes, we have the peace of God. But, we also have the God of peace! When we pray right, think right, and live right then we have the sweet assurance of the presence of God with us. We will know the companionship of the God of peace and, as an added compensation, we will know the influence of the peace of God.

That's what it means to be a big hearted Christian!

CHAPTER SEVENTEEN

The secret to a contented life

My dictionary defines contentment as: "a satisfied state."

Sounds good! The only drawback is that it appears quite elusive. So many are looking for it but end up drawing a blank cheque. They are searching for it but never seem to find it. Their insatiable appetite leads them on one wild goose chase after another, but all they catch is a cold. So many people are discovering today that if something has a price tag attached to it then contentment seems even more distant.

In his book *Simple Faith*, Charles Swindoll cites a poem which expresses the discontent so prevalent in our "I want more" society:

It was spring,
But it was summer I wanted,
The warm days,
And the great outdoors.

It was summer,
But it was autumn I wanted,
The colourful leaves,
And the cool, dry air.

It was autumn,
But it was winter I wanted,
The beautiful snow,
And the joy of the holiday season.

It was winter,
But it was spring I wanted,
The warmth
And the blossoming of nature.

I was a child,
But it was adulthood I wanted.
The freedom, And the respect.

I was 20,
But it was 30 I wanted,
To be mature,
And sophisticated.

I was middle-aged,
But it was 20 I wanted,
The youth,
And the free spirit.

I was retired,
But it was middle age I wanted,
The presence of mind,
Without limitations.

My life was over.
But I never got what I wanted.

What an awful way to live. What a sad way to go. Not satisfied. Not contented. That's what happens when dreams become nightmares and when, like the proverbial dog, we are barking up the wrong tree.

Paul found the secret. Not in things. Not in additives. Not in anything. He discovered contentment in a Person, the Lord Jesus Christ. Contentment can never be found in a safe deposit box. It can be found only in the Lord. When a Christian reduces life to its lowest terms, it's Christ. He is the kernel. Everything else is husk. He, and He alone, is our basis for real contentment.

We can see this working out in Paul's life in the final verses of his upbeat letter to the church at Philippi. There he says, *"I have learned to be content whatever the circumstances"* (4:11). How refreshingly honest. It didn't matter to him if it was hot or cold, wet or dry, or if he was free or fettered, inside or outside, he was plainly contented. When you stop and think about it, that's what makes the difference between him and so many of us.

It's true to say that there are two types of Christians. We are either thermometers or thermostats! You know the difference, don't you?

A thermometer Christian is someone who merely registers what is around him. He doesn't change anything. He just records the prevailing temperature and it's always going up and down.

On the other hand, a thermostat Christian is a person who regulates the atmosphere. They are agents for change and will not be affected by the direction the wind is blowing. They determine policy rather than let the situation dictate to them.

Paul is similar to a thermostat. Spiritually, he wasn't up and down. He wasn't adversely influenced by the things that happened to him. He had a goal in life. He had a mission. He had a clearly defined objective. In every situation he longed for Christ to be magnified.

He would change it before it would change him. That's the kind of man we have here. Someone who influenced others for good. In many ways, he was a catalyst. He is one who precipitated change. Why was he able to act in such a positive manner? He had the security of contentment in his own life. He never saw himself as a victim of his circumstances. He was a victor over them. You see, a man can only do that when his heart is in the right place. He was relaxed. Here is a man at ease with himself rather than someone on the treadmill of self improvement.

This was not a state of euphoria that he happened to fall into overnight nor was it an indifferent couldn't care less attitude. It was something he had learned in the school of life. It is a gradual and progressive experience as one learns to cope with the rough as well as the smooth. He had more than his fair share of problems, enough to give any man stage fright, but he came through in the end with a smile on his face and a story to tell to his followers. How? He developed the ability to accept the situation as it was and he adapted to it. That's the road to contentment.

Contentment actually means "containment." It is an unusual expression but it has the idea of someone who is self-contained. His resources were on the inside and not dependent on substitutes from the outside. The thought is of a person who is self-sufficient. According to Paul's testimony it portrays a man who is at peace in Christ's sufficiency. It's when you believe that He is in total control. Because He lives within us and His power is available to us it means we can face all the demands and pressures of this life. We can cope through Jesus Christ. Our sufficiency is in Him.

So many people go through life thinking that if they could only pack their bags and move upmarket to a new house in a leafy suburb, they would be content. If they could just go to another church which caters for all their needs and those of their family, they would be content. If they could get a new job with better prospects and have the opportunity to make a fresh start, they would be content.

Apparently a man came to the philosopher Socrates on one occasion and asked him about the unhappiness of one of their mutual friends. Socrates answered, "The trouble with that man is that he takes himself with him wherever he goes."

There were a number of factors that contributed to Paul's idyllic feeling of contentment. He was always on the move from A to B and was daily confronted with new challenges and opportunities. Through it all I see a man who is not stressed out and swallowing valium by the handful but a man who is the epitome of contentment, simply satisfied. Why?

HE BELIEVED IN THE PROVIDENCE OF GOD

"I rejoice greatly in the Lord that at last you have renewed your concern for me. Indeed, you have been concerned, but you had no opportunity to show it" (4:10)

One writer makes this fairly ordinary verse come alive with his colourful comments. He says, "Who is saying this? Some young turk who has just turned the deal on his first million? A superstar who recently signed an unbelievable contract? Some guy in his twenties about to set sail on a magnificent adventure? Not on your life. Would you believe, a sixty-plus year old Jew chained to a Roman guard under house arrest, not knowing if tomorrow he will be killed, brought to court, or set free? Though getting up in years, he is rejoicing. Though without the comforts of home and the privileges of privacy, he is happy. Though he doesn't have a clue regarding his future, he is smiling at life. Though he is set aside, forced to stay in one place, completely removed from the excitement of a broader ministry, he is still rejoicing. No matter what happened to him, Paul refused to be caught in the grip of pessimism."

When Paul reflected on his own situation and it dawned upon him that the church at Philippi had shown a measure of love and concern for him just when he needed it most he put it all down to the perfect timing of God. That is providence. This is something we cannot adequately explain. We only know that God is working on our behalf and He orders events so that everything fits perfectly into place. It is the unseen hand of God guiding the hearts of men.

The story of Joseph is a superb illustration of such a truth. His brothers sold him off as a slave. Pride, envy and jealousy got the better of them. The day came, however, when Joseph and his brothers met face to face. When he revealed himself to them, he knew that they would be afraid of him. But Joseph surprised them by looking at his fate from a divine perspective. He told them that they should not be grieved because of what happened, for God had used these events to preserve the lives of multitudes through the preparation that Egypt made for the present famine. Then he summarised his attitude in a single cryptic statement. *"So then, it was not you who sent me here, but God"* (Genesis 45:8).

The theology of Joseph can be summed up in two phrases: "You sold me ... but God sent me!" (cf. Genesis 45:5). He understood that behind the perverse hand of his brothers was the purposeful hand of God. That's providence. He sees events before they happen. He can see the future with precise clarity because He is the One who works events according to His perfect plan. Even while things appear to be out of hand or off course, God is there, working invisibly behind the scenes (cf. Ecclesiastes 7:13,14). Behind a frowning providence God's face is smiling.

No matter what takes place in our lives, as Paul found to his personal pleasure, we can rest in the fact that God is behind the scenes directing the scenes He is behind! It is absolutely thrilling to realise that behind each scene you can see the shadow of the Almighty directing from the wings.

Warren Wiersbe reminds us that "life is not a series of accidents but a series of appointments." So far as the child of God is concerned it's not chance or coincidence. It's not hit and run or even hit and miss. It is certainly not the luck of the draw or picking the shortest straw. Thank God! The abiding principle is enshrined in the unforgettable words of Mordecai, *"And who knows but that you have come to royal position for such a time as this"* (Esther 4:14).

HE WAS IN THE RIGHT PLACE

Paul wasn't living in cloud cuckoo land as he related his own experience of the contented life. For him, the rubber was hitting the road, at times it may have been a bumpy ride but it was always blessed. Let him say it for himself:

"I know what it is to be in need, and I know what it is to have plenty. I have learned the secret of being content in any and every situation, whether well fed or hungry, whether living in plenty or in want" (4:12).

Paul Rees tells the story that years ago, a syndicated column carried the story of a group of famous American financiers who, in the early 1920s had met at the Edgewater Beach Hotel in Chicago. In personal wealth and financial control, they controlled more money than was in the national treasury. From time to time, their names appeared in the press, their influence was enormous, their success fabulous.

Twenty-five years later the columnist called the roll of these princes of the financial world. One of them, a man who had cornered millions through wheat speculation, had died abroad, insolvent. Another, the president of the nation's largest independent steel company, had died penniless. The president of the New York Stock Exchange had recently been released from prison. A member of the cabinet in the Harding administration, after being let out of prison for health reasons, had died at home. The greatest exploiter of the Bear market in Wall Street had committed suicide. The leader of the world's greatest monopoly had also died at his own hand. In summarising the list of men, the writer with remarkable perception said, "All of these men had learned how to make big money, but not one of them had learned how to live."

What a radical difference in the life of Paul. He had learned to live. God never failed him, He never let him down - not once. Yes, there were times when the going was tough as he ran into the wind *and* there were other times when the sun was shining in his face; there were days of poverty *and* there were days of plenty; there were days when money was scarce *and* there were better times when he had so much he didn't know what to do with it; there were meal times when he had to go without and feel the gnawing pangs of hunger *and* there were other occasions when he sat down to a five course feast a la carte.

He was where God wanted him to be. The right place. The right time. And, that's the cue for contentment.

HE FELT THE POWER OF GOD

"I can do everything through Him who gives me strength" (4:13)

This is the ideal motto text for every Christian. We would be hard pressed to find a better watchword for our daily lives. It's not a matter of hangin' in there or holdin' on. It's a vote of confidence in the ability of Jesus. We cannot do it on our own but through Christ we can do it. It means we are continually energised in all things by the strengthening of Christ. He is the One who empowers us so that we are able to operate at maximum efficiency.

That means, when our knees are knocking and our legs feel like jelly, when the butterflies are in the stomach, when we break out in a cold sweat, we can still do whatever task is assigned to us because of the enabling of Jesus.

This is the very essence of Christian living. We can be ready for anything. And, with His strength infused within us, we are able for everything.

He not only gives us the power to live but He is the power for living!

To know the conscious and continual power of the indwelling Christ guarantees the strength to live:

* faithfully (4:1)

* joyfully (4:4)

* helpfully (4:5)

* prayerfully (4:6)

* thankfully (4:6)

* peacefully (4:7)

* thoughtfully (4:8)

HE KNEW THE RIGHT PEOPLE

Paul knows how to motivate people and he does it wonderfully well. He is one of the finest examples of man management around. You only have to read what he says to them about their care and concern for him. He doesn't flatter them. He sincerely thanks them. This epistle is, among other things, a letter of receipt, an acknowledgement of their many love gifts.

"Yet it was good of you to share in my troubles. Moreover, as you Philippians know, in the early days of your acquaintance with the gospel, when I set out from Macedonia, not one church shared with me in the matter of giving and receiving, except you only; for even when I was in Thessalonica, you sent me aid again and again when I was in need. Not that I am looking for a gift, but I am looking for what may be credited to your account. I have received full payment and even more; I am amply supplied, now that I have received from Epaphroditus the gifts you sent. They are a fragrant offering, an acceptable sacrifice, pleasing to God" (4:14-18)

These folks were loyal to the core in their regular support of the apostle. They were not embarrassed when he found himself in trouble and was tossed unceremoniously into prison. No. They kept on giving. It would appear from reading between the lines of what Paul is saying that there were in the early days no other churches involved in his maintenance. The Philippian fellowship seemed to carry the load themselves, and they did so with a heart and a half. And, even when he was ministering in another assembly of the Lord's people, they continued to send him assurances of their love. Here was a local church that gave generously and liberally to the Lord's work through His servant and they prospered spiritually as a result of such noble endeavour.

Charles Swindoll aptly comments: "They never second guessed the apostle in his decision to move on; they supported him. They neither judged him when things went well nor complained when times were hard and he had no fruit to show for his labour; they supported him. They felt pain when he hurt, they prayed for him when he was unable to stay in touch, and they sent friends to comfort him when he was in prison. What a church! No wonder he felt such affection for them."

He just wants them to know how much he is indebted to their practical fellowship. Through them all his needs have been met and all the bills have been paid. And there's even some left over for a rainy day (cf. vs. 18). He is most appreciative of their sacrificial support, prayerfully, financially, every way. He likens their giving to a budding tree in verse 10 and to an investment in verses 14 to 17. It is in verse 18 compared to a fragrant offering with which God is well pleased.

A closer examination of verse 18 would reinforce the truth that the person who is in receipt of the gift is singularly blessed; and the people who give the gift are doubly blessed. And, in a new dimension to giving, God is blessed!

HE STANDS ON THE PROMISE OF GOD

It was Hudson Taylor the founder of the former China Inland Mission (now known as OMF) who coined the phrase: "When God's work is done in God's way for God's glory, it will not lack God's supply." This is the verse he staked his faith on:

"And my God will meet all your needs according to His glorious riches in Christ Jesus" (4:19)

The friends at Philippi had dug deeply into their pockets to meet his needs, in return, they could expect God to look after their many needs.

He would recompense them and they would prove that those who give will always have something to give. Their supplies might be running low but they would never run out! The Philippians had given *out of* their meagre resources but God will give to them *according to* His inexhaustible wealth.

Look at it like this ...

it was personal: "my God"

it was positive: "will meet"

it was pointed: "all your needs"

it was plentiful: "according to His glorious riches"

it was powerful: "in Christ Jesus"

C. H. Spurgeon referred to this verse as the cheque book of the bank of faith. We write in the amount we need, God fills in the rest and signs His name on the dotted line! It never bounces. It's always enough.

Well, that's the last link in the chain to a life of contentment in Christ.

IT'S TIME FOR THE BENEDICTION ...

the glory is for Him

"To our God and Father be glory for ever and ever. Amen." (4:20)

When we invest our lives and our resources in the kingdom of God then He gets the corresponding glory. He deserves it. He is worthy of it. It is rightfully His. It belongs to Him. It is not only for the years of time, but for eternity. The glory will always be ascribed to Him. And, that's the way it should be.

the greetings are for them

"Greet all the saints in Christ Jesus. The brothers who are with me send greetings. All the saints send you greetings, especially those who belong to Caesar's household" (4:21,22)

This is fantastic as it underlines the affinity we share within the family of God. There are three groups of people referred to here. The first group who are with him would probably have included men like Timothy, Dr. Luke, Epaphroditus, Aristarchus from Thessalonica, Tychicus from Asia, and maybe Epaphras the evangelist from Colossae.

The second group is believed by many to have been those whose names were listed in Romans 16. Among them were Ampliatus, Apelles, Stachys, Rufus, Hermes, Tryphena, and Tryphosa. Many of them are relatively unknown to us but each one would be known to those in Philippi.

The final group is the one that has caused most interest over the years. To whom is it referring? Who is included? Could he have in mind the emperor's wife and children bearing in mind that legend has it that while Nero was out of town, his wife listened to the Christian message and turned her life over to Jesus Christ?

This description surely refers to an incredibly large number of people from all over the empire. Since *"all roads lead to Rome"* it would have included slaves, soldiers, senators, men and women of wealth and status, and many others who were drawn to the city and its environs because it was the nerve centre for the expanding empire. There would be those members of the elite Imperial Guard who waited on Caesar doing his special work. And, there would also be those who worked in the corridors of power doing all sorts of jobs.

What thrills me more than anything is that Christ has invaded and infiltrated the very citadel of unbelief. In the very rooms where His name had been an unmentionable, Christ as Lord was now being openly discussed. The inaugural meeting of the Workers Christian Fellowship was probably held there and then. And all of that was happening right under Nero's nose, yet he couldn't stop it! It blows the mind. That's why we give Him all the glory. Yet again, He has brought about an unbelievable ending from an uneventful beginning!

the grace is for you

"The grace of the Lord Jesus Christ be with your spirit" (4:23)

Thus Paul began his letter (cf. 1:2). Thus Paul ended it. It is God's unmerited, unlimited favour that shines upon us all the time along all the way. It is grace that set our feet on the highway to heaven. It is grace that keeps us company all the journey through. It is grace that will see us safely home at last.

What a marvellous way to end a letter. *"Amen"* is what he says. And, so say all of us!

That's it! Paul has nothing more to say. He rolled up the scroll and gave it to his friend Epaphroditus. They prayed together. Paul bade him a fond farewell as he knew their paths would never cross again this side of glory. He journeyed home to Philippi with the letter in his pocket. When he arrived he gathered the church together and they heard what Paul had to say for the first time. The pastor read it again ... and again ... and again. They got the message! Have you? There's joy in Jesus!